at HOME & at WORK

at HOME & at WORK

architects' and designers' empowered spaces

Carol Soucek King, Ph.D.

An Imprint of

PBC INTERNATIONAL, INC.

Distributor to the book trade in the United States and Canada:

Rizzoli International Publications Inc.
300 Park Avenue South
New York, NY 10010

Distributor to the art trade in the United States and Canada:

PBC International, Inc.
One School Street
Glen Cove, NY 11542
1-800-527-2826
Fax 516-676-2738

Distributor throughout the rest of the world:

Hearst Books International
1350 Avenue of the Americas
New York, NY 10019

Library of Congress Cataloging-in-Publication Data

King, Carol Soucek.
    At home and at work : architects' & designers' empowered spaces /
by Carol Soucek King.
       p.   cm.
    Originally published as: Empowered spaces.
    Includes index.
    ISBN 0-86636-249-5 (domestic trade version)
    1. Architecture--Psychological aspects.   2. Architects-
-Interviews.   3. Interior decoration--Psychological aspects.
4. Interior designers--Interviews.   I. Soucek King, Carol.
Empowered spaces.   II. Title.
NA2540.S58   1993
720'.1'9--dc20   93-18655
                                                                    CIP

CAVEAT—Information in this text is believed accurate, and will pose no
problem for the student or casual reader. However, the author was often
constrained by information contained in signed release forms, information
that could have been in error or not included at all. Any misinformation (or
lack of information) is the result of failure in these attestations. The author
has done whatever is possible to insure accuracy.

Color separation by Fine Arts Repro House Co., Ltd.
Printing and binding by Toppan Printing Co.

Printed in China

Typography by
TypeLink, Inc.

10 9 8 7 6 5 4 3 2 1

With my gratitude to all those who have empowered me, most especially…

My husband Richard King, with whose support and love I feel I could do anything.

Romus and Anne Soucek, whom I had the unbelievably good fortune to land as parents, and the late Commander Philip Merrill Soucek, USN, my true blue brother.

My extraordinarily elegant grandmother Estelle Merrill Boyce and her husband William Alexander Boyce, M.D., who believed in me.

My mentors Dr. Laurence E. Morehouse and his wife Thelma Morehouse.

The caring Herbert F. Sturdy, Herbert Linden, Herbert Stahl, Ph.D., Dr. and Mrs. Merrill Winsett, and Mr. and Mrs. Charles Schmidt.

The inspirational Ray Bradbury.

This book's editor Kevin Clark to whom the idea of focusing on architects' and interior designers' own homes and offices first occurred, Joanne Caggiano for her organizational and administrative help, and Mark Serchuck and Penny Sibal, for seeing a need to produce this book.

My gifted associates at *Designers West/Designers World:* Rick Eng, Angeline Vogl, Keli Dugger, and the generous Susan Pomrantz without whose constant help and buoyant spirit this book would not have been possible.

My great friend Walton E. Brown, publisher of *Designers West* and *Designers World* magazines through whose pages I have been allowed entry into so many empowered spaces.

TABLE OF CONTENTS

Throughout life, in order for us to communicate who we really are, we must make the most of our tools. The result of this ability, once gained, is power...the power to represent and reinforce who we are today and who we want to be.

The following chapters are based on visits with sixty architects and interior designers, some already world leaders in their field, others just beginning to leave their mark. Through developed skills and a refined sense of their own individual character, these professionals have molded the environments in which they live and work into clear projections of their own personal and public identities.

Through these professionals it becomes evident that what one considers a powerful space is highly personal, with as many interpretations as there are individuals. However, there is one common thread running throughout everything they say and practice: the realization that the truly powerful space is the result of organized and deeply felt emotion. It is that perspective which is necessary for those who would enliven space and empower it.

The ability of these professionals to be intimately in touch with their innermost creative selves has enabled them to find truth when expressing themselves through their environments. In fact, they expressed themselves with such brilliant clarity, even when de-scribing what it is they do, that they changed somewhat my approach in undertaking this work. When I first began the series of interviews that would make up this collection, I had assumed I would turn them into the typical descriptive type of article in which the subjects' quotes are used only intermittently. As I progressed, however, I found that what they had to say was expressed with so much individuality and came so directly from the heart that I decided to interfere as little as possible. It was privilege enough to try to put their ideas down on paper with the same sort of directness that they had been given to me. In doing so, I have hoped to serve primarily as recorder, passing along the wisdom of finely tuned professionals who are also artists...aware of what they have accomplished and eager to go further still.

As they describe the environments in which they live and work, as well as explain their design philosophy in general, other design industry professionals will find this book filled with insight. But it is intended as an inspirational guide for all who are interested in extending their understanding of the degree to which personal space can be made useful and expressive.

I myself have felt highly motivated and continually uplifted by what these architects and designers have conveyed. May the reader feel the same.

Carol Soucek King

the Explorers

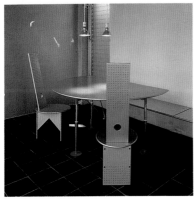

David Weingarten and Lucia Howard

at work & at home

Contemporary ideas of places that inspire creativity are based on a heroic, abstract, minimalist model. Expanses of unadorned white surfaces, drenched in sunlight, surround a lone artist poised before an unmarked canvas/page/stone, the tabula rasa, ready to receive the impression of solitary genius. In this setting, distraction in its various guises as figuration, personal history, and other human beings are kept at bay, so that the artistic impulse will be undisturbed. In the abstract glory of this setting, the artist is freed to confront, as if for the first time, the great problems of his art.

The places our firm Ace Architects designs for itself, both home and studio, must be based on some other model. The settings we like the best (those to which we aspire) and which encourage us architecturally are jam-packed with distractions, traces of history, and souvenirs inciting memory. We far prefer John Soane's apartment in London, Elvis' Graceland in Memphis, or any house overwhelmingly redolent of its occupant, to places which are spare, cool, neutral, and anonymous, no matter how elegant.

For us, it is the singularly over-wrought space, rather than the undifferentiated, that is most congenial to creativity. Nearly all our work occurs in places we have designed for ourselves. By contrast, our edge dulls in airplanes, airports, hotel rooms, the entire range of generic environments. Without the use of our own eccentric and idiosyncratic places, Ace would be in deep water, creativity-wise.

David's home on Darrell Place in San Francisco is imagined as a figurative reconstruction of the history of the Bay Region Style. The main floor is modeled on a nineteenth-century library by John Soane, recast in Bay Regional materials, a typical device of the First Bay Region Style. The building's most architectural space is its study, the Architecture Room. A perfect cube, the room is a vivid yellow with identical arches and flanking niches on each wall. A ceiling mural depicts the cycle of the Bay Region Styles, symbolized by architects holding models of their most influential buildings around the base of a domed roof. The room houses collections of metal building replicas, etchings by Piranesi, and architectural books.

Leviathan, the home of Ace Architects, is a new four-story office building on the Oakland waterfront. We imagined a coppery green sea monster draped over a gray naval vessel forward and a red and white checked supertanker aft. Topside are a drafting room in the creature's belly, and the partners' offices within its brain. Metal ribs in the drafting room glisten beneath tall monitors. A copper stair at one end leads to the dome-covered brain above. Bilaterally symmetrical, the head contains the bone structure for the creature's eyes, nose, mouth, and spinal column. Windows fill the eye sockets, and the door in its mouth gives onto a lookout platform atop the creature's tentacles. This room is designed as the place for us to design, and here our most intensely creative work occurs.

Stylistically, Darrell Place and Leviathan are very different. Darrell Place is conceived in the language of traditional architecture, while Leviathan's vocabulary is Modern. Darrell Place is about architecture. It is dense with references to other architects and architectural elements that refer to other buildings. Leviathan is not about buildings at all. Its design sources are sea creatures, maritime machinery, ships, and stories of the sea.

Yet the two have much in common. Both are literal in the way they render their subjects, the sources for their design. Both are evocative and suggestive, provoking memories and fantasies. Neither subscribes to the view of architecture as a somber, serious subject. Our buildings are meant to be fun and to be enjoyed, and sometimes to entertain.

Our creative juices flow most freely in the settings that are richest to us—our own home and studio. Loaded with meanings and memories, these settings embody not only ideas and associations, but also the history of their own making. The experiences of construction, the successes and disappointments, battles, and surprises of each part of the building lend it an aura that only its designers see.

The relationship between a rich setting and creativity is analogous to that between a rich context and interesting architecture. A powerful and complex context, including not just the physical setting but also relevant history and ideas, is often a pre-condition of the best architecture. The most familiar jampacked settings, those that hold associations and memories *for us,* provoke our best and most highly charged work.

top

With chairs from Cardinal Rizzonico's dinette, a set of colorful plywood chairs and table by Ace. The background is the wall of the office library covered in copper shingles.

top right

Leviathan, the home of Ace Architects, which we imagined a coppery green sea monster draped over a gray naval vessel forward and a red and white checked supertanker aft.

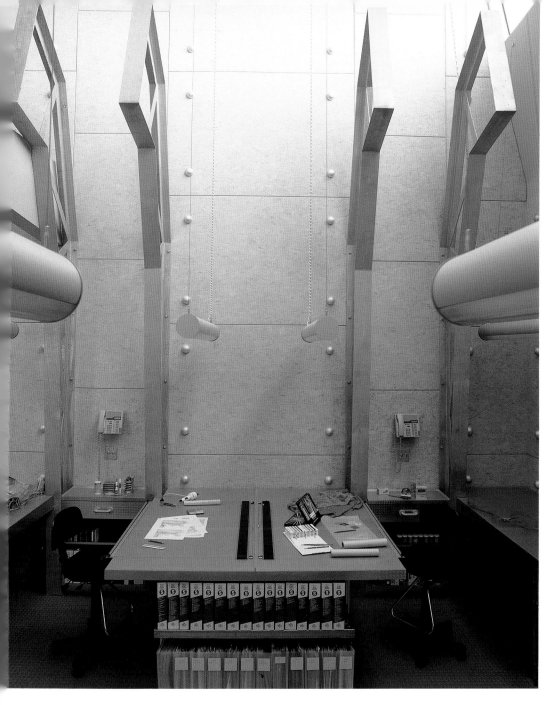

top right

The corridor outside our offices continues the color and mythology of the exterior.

top left & opposite

Metal ribs in the drafting room glisten beneath tall monitors. A copper stair at one end leads to the dome-covered brain above.

left

The Bay Bridge is viewed beyond my personal collection including a nineteenth-century Chinese export chair, a nineteenth-century stone griffin from the Houses of Parliament, cobra-headed rails and fire tools forged by John Fick, and a collection of Day of the Dead papier-mâché skulls and musicians.

top right

A ceiling mural with the history of the Bay Region Style by Judy Choi, a late eighteenth-century American round table that converts to a chair, as well as various metal and ceramic building replicas and souvenirs are at home in the Architecture Room.

bottom right

At my Darrell Place condominium, a statue of the *Muse of Architecture* looks toward the kitchen island, shaped like the room in miniature, with the model of an early twentieth-century American Southern style house above.

Rand Elliott

at home

Photography by Michael Ives

Our lives are so hectic, so filled with tension, that to us our home's most important aspect is its sparse serenity. Indeed, the goal I share with my wife Jeanette is to have little or no furniture at all. My designs are always direct and unencumbered by the unnecessary and meaningless. Besides, I've never been afraid of stepping out on a limb and doing something different.

The concept we developed for our home is "ghosts"…the ghosts of the previous owners, the lives lived here, the memories of earlier times. As an active historic preservationist, I enjoy keeping the past of our home alive. We take pleasure in its being situated in a historical preservation area near downtown Oklahoma City, and are intrigued by its having been built in 1920 by one of the city's early civic leaders to reflect the Italianate style he himself had grown to admire while on a transatlantic voyage.

I feast on all these underpinnings of my current habitat and incorporate some of its historic detailing in my designs, with a few personal twists. The house is a laboratory, a place where I can experiment with lighting and products, where I can do what I want. I change it all the time.

Our "ghost" concept is promoted via the use of white paint, luminous and translucent materials, fragments of the original structure, and light. Every room is a space painted with light, where new and old live together in harmonious contrast and appreciation. The old is embellished, while the new takes on a fresh new energy.

The home's entry sets the tone for the "ghost" concept to unfold. A second entry door once concealed with plaster has been uncovered, its opening now an infill panel floating in an ice-like outline. This "iced" acrylic process, which I patented, is used extensively throughout the house, its shadowy and translucent quality being central to the ghostly illusion. Other-worldly, too, is the entire entry floor; we discovered the original oak beneath a layer of tired asphalt tile, now moon-splashed with light patterns from framing projectors above. Adjacent spotlights make the imported Italian plaster angels seem to soar.

Little has changed in the living area, beyond new low voltage lighting, white paint and whitened oak floors. The crown and door moldings are original,

top left

I and my ghosts.

top right

In the entry, a 1953 drawing by French architect Le Corbusier hangs on a panel, existing iron levers remain on the doors. The stair is original and seems to have been inspired by Charles Rennie Mackintosh. Best of all, this and every door in the house is adorned by a small plaster bell, the romantic signature of the original owner whose name was Bell.

as are the fireplace carvings which have been left in their original condition and color. Gas logs have been replaced by a sculptural glass screen designed by Marilynn Adams to reflect the Zen-like energy of the space.

The dining room, with its softly illuminated carved wood molding and plaster wedding cake ceiling, is presented as art in and of itself. Nothing but five recessed glass test tubes with their single floral specimens adorn the "ice sculpture" dining table.

I tried to rethink what a kitchen is all about and conceived it more as sculpture than the usual functional room. I used cabinets made of "iced" acrylic. They appear to be translucent towers. Against their soft white luminosity, even the hinges take on a ghost-like quality. Above the Japanese tile floor with its curving bottom edge, base cabinets seem to float. Flowing plastic splash plates that overlap the windows beyond, ice-like bi-fold doors separating the kitchen from the utility room, even the web-like extensions of the twelve-volt wire light system carry forth the "ghostly" theme.

The center island is a twelve-foot long granite countertop terminating with a three-foot diameter black disc. This is the center of energy for the entire house, the place where people like to hang out.

"Broken" openings, created throughout the house—between living area, kitchen and staircase—indicate that these new openings are not original, and wood wall studs on the floor reveal the location of the original walls, more ghosts of the past.

An art gallery concept for the upstairs hallway includes pieces of mirror on the floor, illuminated from above to create a wall of refracted light.

The master bedroom combines two bedrooms from the first owner's plan, again the result showing original studs on the floors.

I always believe your life will be better when you're surrounded by design that is meaningful to you personally. Your life will be uplifted, and things don't have to be expensive to be good. My life is uplifted by this space.

top left

The upstairs hallway, now an art gallery, captures refracted light from a broken mirror.

top right

The once old-fashioned master bath is now an island of ice-like forms.

bottom left

Nothing is allowed to disturb the original "wedding cake" molding of the dining room. Only a sculptured dining table is added, with its five recessed test tube floral receptacles.

opposite

In the kitchen, ice-like acrylic extends the ghostly metaphor, while a disk of black granite defines the family's central gathering place.

Little has changed in the living area beyond low voltage lighting, white paint and whitened oak floors. The original sun porch beyond has been converted into a music room with eight pairs of operable French windows. In contrast, wall lights are fashioned from a wall-mounted electrical box, a slab of the ice material, a coil cord and a bare lamp. Marilynn Adams' sculptural glass screen reflects the Zen-like energy of the space.

at home

When walls were removed in the master bedroom, original studs were revealed and today look like works of art on the floor.

All photography by Shinkenchiku-sha

Toyo Ito
at home

In the process of designing "Silver Hut," my own house in Tokyo, I was deeply conscious of creating a natural and primitive state for architecture within the possibilities of modern technology. Before, I was obsessed with the formalistic approach to architecture, but I came to realize that architecture should free itself from taking on a critical character.

One would wonder if there would be any kind of possibility of a primitive structure which would replace the traditional primitive hut and fit in the contemporary city. Since I did not come up with a definite answer, my process was rather one of elimination. I did not use a concrete vault because it would carry with it various significant and historical meanings, or a full-circle vault, as it would be too heavy, so I made it more shallow. In contrast to the traditional primitive hut made of wood, it seemed more natural to use light steel in contemporary Tokyo, so as not to overload this house with former meanings. However, I have incorporated some old materials from our previous house since I wanted to maintain some memories from the old house. Therefore, parts of the former house were put under the frame of the "Silver Hut." *Kawara*, Japanese roof tile, *shoji* screens, even the *tokobashira* (the wooden post from the *tokonoma* area) were introduced to this new house. On the other hand, I also used plenty of materials, particularly aluminum, so that these elements would not overly emphasize the image of the old house. While these metals create technological lightness and give a spaceship feeling to it, this house also evokes a feeling of *doma* (a space for cooking and domestic work, the plan of which developed naturally from reflecting the behavioral needs of the inhabitants) of the traditional Japanese house.

It is interesting for me that the contrast of these two opposite images are derived by nature working as intermediary. These images of this house somewhat reflect the aspects of the contemporary city. I believe that it would be more natural for architecture to reflect new aspects of modern life. Therefore, my intention was to avoid a particular style which was already sanctified, recognized and perfected. In the midst of Tokyo, which is probably the most dynamic city in the world, I am in search of a primitive and natural architecture. I want to be new, but at the same time simple.

top left

In my courtyard

top right

South side of the courtyard

bottom right

Evening view from south

opposite

Kitchen

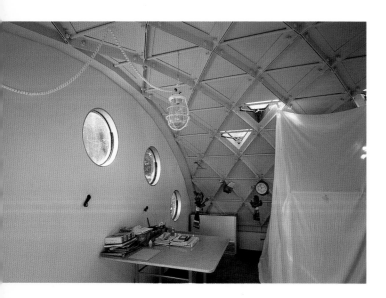

top

Children's room on
second floor

bottom

Dining room

right

Courtyard

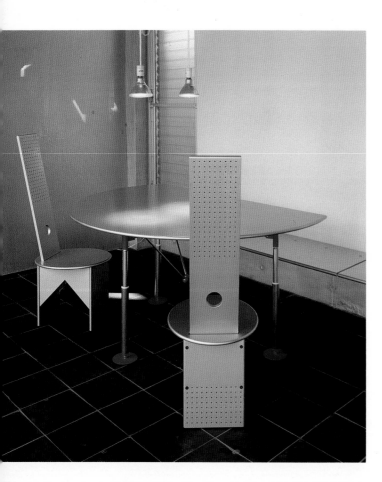

Photography by Toshi Yoshimi

Cleo Baldon
at work & at home

Photography by Jim McHugh

At first when asked about my own pool, I think only of the extreme pleasure of that first gliding stroke pushing off into that long slit of teal blue water. There's a comforting, protected quality in swimming along a long narrow (eight feet, three inches) channel, this one lined with Idaho quartz stone that also runs through my native Washington and strews the banks of my childhood lake with its micro-flaked sparkle. The fountain is an old Italian marble and bronze thing that my husband, Ib Melchior, inherited from his father. The whole of it is an improbably narrow side yard only twenty feet wide in all, the pool eight feet from the house. Being that close to the house, the lighted pool at night is a magic light to the dining room. The raised pool, at bench height, gives us forty feet of free furniture. The fish pond at the end, that only appears to be filled by pool water, is right outside the kitchen door which forces us to enjoy it

Photography © Julius Shulman, Hon. AIA

top left

With my partner Sid Galper, at Galper/ Baldon Associates, Venice, California.

top right

Water is our material, but at the office we had to understand how to come to grips with the ocean…how to let it in and also keep its powerful glare out.

bottom left

For Sid Galper, my partner, we gambled on being able to swim a long thin curve….

bottom right

If we have afforded as much pleasure to our clients as we have at my house it's a worthy life.

opposite

We turn inward around a tree-dominated space.

Photography by Mark Schwartz

coming and going. If we have afforded as much pleasure to our clients as we have at my house it's a worthy life.

When we designed a pool for Sid Galper, my partner, we gambled on being able to swim a long thin curve. You can, easily, and it's an adventure. So that's what two planners of pools did for themselves.

Water is our material and our interest and a whole long ocean of it stretching outside our office window is an important element of our lives. Fortunately, we used the building for a while before we started remodeling, and I began to understand how to come to terms with the ocean—the obtrusive, powerful glare of it, letting it in and keeping it out, and also the circus that is Venice, California, letting it in and keeping it out. We turn inward around a tree-dominated space.

Bart Prince
at home

I remember realizing as a child that music and architecture, both of which captured my devotion early on, are complete art forms. Each has rhythm, form, and uses a combination of instruments or materials. I always intended to be an architect; I was always drawing, and even won an award when I was seven and built my first building when I was fifteen. But, I started studying music when I was seven also, and in my mind they became inseparable.

To me, working and living at the same place is an ideal composition for one's life...if you love what you do. It gives your life composure, makes it integral. I feel like Frank Lloyd Wright when he said "my office is under my hat." Sometimes, I work all day and night without stopping, and having my studio a part of my home enables my existence to be more of one piece. I have another location nearby where the engineering for our projects is done, but usually for my own work a couple of assistants come here. Since I don't take on more work than I can personally do myself—usually some four to six projects at various stages—this is very harmonious.

My office is my home. Although I am always pleased to have clients visit my home, it's not a showplace. It's for my work and for me alone. It's a physical representation of my design philosophy, but it wasn't intended to be my design statement, something by which I could market myself as an architect. These days in architecture there are far too many ineffectual word games that have nothing to do with reality...or comfort...or the total expression of a person's needs. They are just a bunch of nonsense. A house, my house, is not a metaphor, it's an organic idéa. The design grows from a need, it grows from the inside out and becomes whatever it needs to become.

Oftentimes, the designer has an image in mind, something he is trying to arrive at and he works back and forth, trying to satisfy that image, regardless of how illogical it is. I never do. I start from the inside, from the requirements, the relationships of the parts to the site...the sun...the functional aspects...and then the design begins to grow. This becomes the physical structure, and it has integrity.

In planning my home, I had a long narrow site in an old neighborhood in Albuquerque, the city where I grew up. There is one long side facing generally

to the south, and I decided I wanted sun coming into every space. Another consideration was a noisy street on one end, with the long side being on a quieter street. So, I used the studio as a buffer toward the noisy end, and placed the more private living room area at the other end. Acoustics are always important to me, as I seek quiet for my reading, my music and my private life. So, to avoid noise further, I wanted to raise the bedroom and smaller chamber type rooms. This also provided a view for those areas. The space between was used for additional outside deck area.

Since these photographs were taken, I've built a tower for a library and incorporated a waterfall. I built the tower because my library is constantly growing, with some rare books and drawings for which I needed a more protected space. So this, too, developed from a real need, as did places upstairs and down for my pianos.

Additionally, my use of materials develops from need. I've always believed architecture should be expressive of its own time which leads naturally to my involving new ways to use materials and new ways to think about space. I grew up in more ordinary types of buildings, adobes, which were fine. But, I remember thinking as a child that they were dark and cramped and had nothing to do with modern life. I saw nothing wrong with the natural materials. It was just that the use of them seemed outdated.

In this house, there is really nothing that in and of itself is unusual in terms of materials; just the way they are used and the way they are combined with other materials seems surprising. I used regular pipes for the structural beams, then spanned between those with wood

for the decking. They are both ordinary materials, but the shapes they create and the way they are put together are unusual. In the same way it is the placement of the concrete cylinders, not the concrete cylinders themselves—that is unusual—the way they come around the house and are arranged in relationship to each other, not vertically but leaning inward and at varying heights. These are readily available materials, but used unconventionally. Yet, the choice of such materials and the ways they are used, like all of my designs, evolved organically according to my requirements, not arbitrarily.

Another influence in my home is that it reflects my attempt to live simply. Being expressive doesn't need to be expensive. In this house, we have achieved a lot with a small financial investment, and this is an idea I have been able to carry forth in many of my projects.

In addition, a major consideration is

Opposite
The library.

scale. I am always thinking from the point of view that a building is going to be used by humans, and try to understand anew what that really means. I place myself in the space and imagine what it would feel like, what the transition from one place to another would be like, as opposed to having a preconceived idea of space that, once built, we'll cram everything into it.

Varying scale is important to me, too. I compare it to changing tempo in music. The ceilings in my home range from eight to twenty feet. I also think there's a quality of mystery and surprise in music that should exist in architecture as well. That's why I don't like too much explanation. I think you can learn about architecture through listening to music, and vice versa. Or, the architect might gain inspiration from reading a poem. But, you can't translate architecture into words any more than you can translate music.

opposite

My studio in my home.

top

A passageway between my studio and deck. Architecture should have surprises.

bottom

You can't translate architecture into words anymore than you can translate music. But, each can learn from the other, and there are similarities in value, scale and composition.

George Yabu and Glenn Pushelberg

at work

Photography by David Whittaker

Pushelberg

At Yabu Pushelberg we do not have a set approach to our work and do not follow an exclusive doctrine. We believe in innate sensitivity, and we try to think intuitively. By relying on ourselves, we hope to create unique answers for each client and each design problem...answers that will tap people's emotions. To reach people emotionally requires a highly individual approach to each project. Perhaps being located in Toronto helps us. Because Canada is not perceived as having a strong design image, others don't have the tendency to impose preconceived attitudes upon us. We can begin our thought process on a clean canvas.

How we achieve this varies. For instance, we enjoy investigating old materials and applying new meanings...we like to continually reinvent ourselves. Perhaps that is the reason we are working more with low technology...like operating the doors in our studio with counterweights. As the world continues to become slicker, faster and more complex, we too often forget our past, how basic, fundamental materials look or how old processes worked. To us, they are fascinating. We particularly enjoy taking mundane objects out of their usual context and using them in unexpected ways.

top left

Glenn Pushelberg and George Yabu.

top right

Entry Hall—tranquil and Zen-like in mood.

bottom

Door to presentation area and gallery/ conference room a multi-purpose exhibition/ display and meeting area that can be opened up or divided into three individual zones.

Yabu

We take off-the-shelf or catalog items and use them in fresh ways. Examples are the general service lights we used in the otherwise clean spaces of the studio, and the chipboard we stained, sealed and installed as panels looks really elegant. The floor, which appears to some like marble, is actually polished sandstone. Of course, it was particularly important to us in our studio not to use luxurious materials, instead to experiment and work with the more prosaic. We have a reputation for experimenting and taking chances, and it is helpful to our clients to be able to see the results of our explorations here. It was equally important in designing our studio that we not come across as having a singular style. Alternately, our working space reflects a highly exploratory approach, which is a message to be transmitted to our clients as well as to our design team working here. It is an environment that is inviting and calm, yet conceivably, stimulating and provocative as well.

The only thing that is important about fads and trends is to understand them well enough so that you can stay away from them. They have nothing to do with defining a unique and worthwhile approach. Researching new materials and networking with other designers, manufacturers and architects has everything to do with good design, and these activities must be pursued throughout the world. Too often, if you don't keep up with what is happening elsewhere, you too easily settle for what's easy and near-at-hand. You have to look beyond your local environment, you have to travel, see the world and strive to continually relearn and rethink your profession.

Pushelberg

When you do that persistently, you tend to embrace the necessities of the time...not its trends. For example, becoming less wasteful in your use of materials and avoiding irreplaceable woods evolves naturally as a part of your program, because you've kept yourself in tune with significant movements and their consequences. Being creative is not a premeditated thing. It's a matter of exposing oneself and one's staff to as much as possible, whether through reading or encouraging clients to let the staff visit a project site. It's extremely important that designers be highly versed about design and its consequences.

If a designer does have a lot to say, it should be evident in his or her own environment. If designers truly believe that design enhances life, their own environment should express it.

Yabu

Of course, when we started out, we didn't have the chance to create a home for ourselves. Now that we have, we appreciate it every day. We can feel the soul, the passion of all that we've done here. It invigorates us, it is an extremely positive environment for our clients and ourselves, and it has become a place that people enjoy.

top

Corridor connecting reception area and studio with view to administrative work station.

bottom left

Guest bathroom with a spiralling shower on a platform, which contains any wetness without the need of a door.

bottom right

Hall to studio from reception: A generous breathing space before entering the studio.

Studio, with rigging-
supported partitions.
Fully integrated wiring
for power and
communication with
some character not
found in today's
manufactured systems.

George Yabu and Glenn Pushelberg ● at work

Steven Ehrlich
at home

top left

Julia (pink dress), now five years old, Vanessa, eleven, Marlo and Steven. This family portrait supports the strong indoor-outdoor connections so fundamentally a part of this house.

top right

By maintaining a series of large existing trees (encouraged by landscape designer Jay Griffeth), the light and mass of the residence is camouflaged from the residential street. The cubistic play of masses is enhanced by the contrast of pure and direct materials, including burnished grey concrete stucco, clear glass and black stainless steel from Japan, here used for the first time in the United States.

opposite

In this single and pure space we were very conscious of how large qualities of soft light are brought in to wash large art walls. The work above the fireplace is by artist John Okulick. The couch is plywood and was designed by myself. The "zebra" chair is by Alvar Aalto. The mohair custom couch I designed with my wife Marlo.

One of my main objectives in building our home was to put my family into a stronger and more meaningful connection with nature. This introspective quality replenishes the soul and reinforces the family.

Our three thousand three hundred square foot residence in Santa Monica Canyon, California, emanated from an existing single story twelve hundred square foot cottage nestled into a fifty-foot by one-hundred-and-forty foot hillside lot in a suburban neighborhood.

The liberating concept was the realization that the main public activities should occur on the upper floors in order to take advantage of the light and view. Furthermore, by cutting a terrace into the hill, a yard was created. The pedestal for this on the ground level is created by three bedrooms, two of which (for the children) are vestiges of the original house.

Each of the three stories is in dialogue with the terraced hillside, together they form a courtyard house. Every level connects to the ground for a strong indoor-outdoor relationship. Massing of the spaces is peeled back to create an open proportion for the multilevel courtyard.

The house is bisected by a three-story circulation atrium which contains the stairs and principal circulation. This, on ground level, bisects the children's bedrooms from the master and, on the second level, the kitchen/family area from the more formal living/dining space. A dumbwaiter serves the kitchen from the garage two floors below.

All three levels connect with terraces and bridges to the hillside, with its lushly landscaped cascade of greenery over white concrete walls. We live in harmony with our own mini-Hollywood Bowl.

Photography by Scot Zimmerman

graphy by Claudio Santini

top

This is the main atrium space through which the two stairways and, thus, vertical circulation occur. The skylight space is further animated by the kinetic sculpture by light artist Michael Hayden. In the daytime, the sun refracts prism colors through it. At night, the sculpture and space are further enlivened by blue and red moving neon.

bottom left

This bathroom is a hedonistic view of a spartan lifestyle. The pedestal sink, designed by Marlo Ehrlich, is made of chrome supports and veined black marble.

bottom right

Glass handrails are "invisible" and baby-proof at the same time.

Photography by Lawrence Manning

Photography by Scot Zimmerman

top left

I have always been interested in the play of light and dance of shadows, and this was emphasized when I lived in Africa for six years. Here, the frosted glass serves multiple purposes: a screen for casting shadows, a visual barrier increasing privacy on the side yard, and a backdrop and niche for floral arrangements.

Antoine Predock

at work & at home

For twenty-two years I have lived and worked in one place in Albuquerque, New Mexico. I couldn't do it any other way; since my life is my work, it's all one experience. I also have a small studio and living space in Venice, California, and, although these are not physically at one site, they are only a two-minute ride from each other. Here in Albuquerque, however, my studios wrap around my house...private studios where I work by myself and studios that the staff and I share.

The office and my home are both located in pre-existing buildings. We work in old warehouses dating back to the early 1940s. My home is a 1906 bungalow. So we in fact had three disparate buildings that had nothing to do with each other. I linked them together via courtyards, so it is actually a desert compound with lots of hard surfaces—brick and white stucco walls—cooled by fountains. It is a desert place, and over the years I have continued to refine it.

The work spaces are separated from my living spaces by a sequence of these courtyards, some very lush and some austere and dry. For example, one with shade is where we make models. Respecting the indoor-outdoor possibilities is important in this land of climatic extremes.

The approach to my studio offers a sense of mystery and expectation because you don't know what's behind the wall. It is anonymous from the street, but when you get into the space, you understand how the courtyards work to create microcosms of nature and to respond to seasonal change. Each area is used actively for luncheons and staff meetings.

· The idea of physically combining life and work is important to me because I don't think I could function properly if I were commuting. It would be very artificial because everything in my life is fueled by my work. I don't mean that all I ever do is work—I'm very active athletically and from this base here I have great access to bicycling paths that meander along the Rio Grande and through downtown and Old Town.

Being in the Rio Grande Valley roots me in the original energies of this place. Many cultural memories go back to the earliest use by the Indians of this land, and on through the period of Hispanic occupation and colonization, to

the Anglo period. So, there is quite a vivid mixture of cultures living here. It is not like being in some American city that has no feeling of roots, and so many are so young and so rootless. Of course, that can be interesting, too—the idea of being raw and still growing. There are parts of Albuquerque that still are like that.

Still, it is the cultural admixture that interests me, and this inevitably influences my architecture, inasmuch as I view architecture as an all-inclusive art even though my own work is very gestural. This comes perhaps from the clay models and artifacts I make and possibly from my having studied painting in the 1960s. It all contributes to the atmosphere here being not that of a business, but much more that of a studio. Obviously, however, with a staff of twenty-five this is very much a business and very demanding.

Although I could just as well have situated my main office in New York or Los Angeles if I were only considering my clientele, I chose to live here because my own roots are here. I feel very much connected with its spirit, with its extraordinary geography. Everything at this five-thousand-foot elevation can be seen far and wide through a rarified light. The sense of the power of the land is unsurpassed by any place I have ever experienced, and it has had an indelible influence on my own spirit and on what I create.

top right

Front elevation of office and house.

left

Model room, dominated at the time this photograph was taken by a model of The American Heritage Center/Art Museum, University of Wyoming, Laramie.

bottom

Private work area.

Photography by Martin Cohen

Barbara Lazaroff
at home

Photography by Martin Cohen

I believe the essential "secret" of the creative mind is being open to all stimuli—travel, conversation, introspection, the arts, great food and wine, and nature—for all experiences support and stimulate the designing spirit. I adhere to a few basic tenets that apply to my work and my life. I am so fond of one that I had it engraved on a huge boulder in front of our restaurant, Granita, "Time is meaningless in the face of creativity." Another personal by-law is "More is more, less is less." Perhaps a fabulous quote by film critic Pauline Kahl helps me explain this philosophy. It includes the sad revelation of how our society views art and the people who create it: "In this country we encourage 'creativity' among the mediocre, but real bursting creativity appalls us. We put it down as undisciplined, as somehow 'too much.'...Art doesn't come in measured quantities: it's got to be too much or it's not enough."

I was always thought of as the "artistic child." I responded to the play of light and dark so intensely that my earliest memory at merely fifteen months of age is a silhouette of my mother, backlit, returning from the hospital with my newborn brother. Color, texture and form had strong emotional effects on me; as a child I was constantly cutting, gluing and painting. On many occasions, family members would find themselves tripping over the furniture I had rearranged in the middle of the night. My family always lived in somewhat confined quarters. Our apartment was so small that I slept in a room with two brothers almost until I left for college. My earliest fantasies were of large open spaces and gardens filled with flowers of intense colors. I craved the world of museums and magical palaces, and yet I also yearned to be a cowgirl riding the open prairies surveying my ranch filled with a "Noah's Ark" of animals—especially a llama. Most of this paradox of ambitions has come true, even the llama. In fact I have two.

Even though I was considered the bohemian of the family, ironically, after my first two years of studying lighting for the theater and stage design, I spent the next ten years of my university level education concentrating on the study of biochemistry and experimental psychology with the intent of becoming a neuroendocrinologist. My early life experiences, life circumstances, and these disparate elements in my later studies are the basis of who I am, how I work, and how I realize and bring to fruition my "imaginings." I believe my training as a scientist has taught me patience and persistence and this has helped me in the problem-solving phase of design. My empirical knowledge of the operational aspects of restaurants has aided me as well, in terms of space planning, maintenance, cost, efficiency, and issues such as what the patron and the employee need and desire.

Over the years, many of the lessons I have learned, discoveries I have made, and the relationships with craftspeople and artisans I have formed have slowly been incorporated into my home. Six years ago I purchased a large, traditional English Tudor home, this architecture being the one that most closely fit my childhood perception of what a house should look like. Ironically, I have decorated almost all of the interior with contemporary furniture and art—once again the paradox of my moods arises. Only the garden areas with their multileveled cascading stone steps and English flower beds echo the sensibility of the historical architecture. I believe the creation of one's home environment is an ongoing, dynamic process. A home is never "finished" by virtue of one's ever-changing and evolving life and living experiences. Both in my home and in my restaurant spaces—which indeed are also very much my home (I often spend more time in the restaurants that I created for myself than I do in my actual domicile), I want to create an element of magic and fantasy and yet it has to still be functional and comfortable. In addition, the reality of day-to-day usage, the maintenance of a menagerie of twenty-eight animals and a very active three-and-a-half year old, have taught me a sense of leniency about the "perfection of the space."

Prior to the birth of my son Cameron, I built a design studio in my home, with doors that open to a garden of nearly four hundred rose bushes—the majority are over forty five years old and they are priceless in their beauty and in the joy they give me. Above the studio I've built a large play area for Cameron. Sometimes, if I'm overwhelmed or stymied, I listen to his laughter or I exit my studio through the garden side and come up and paint or squeeze a little Play Dough with him—it's a great refresher. When I really need to "get away" while working, I take my drafting table out to the llama area. The only drawback to that is on occasion they have eaten a few of my "tastier" fabric samples.

In the six years that I have owned this home, I've spent the majority of it on job-sites building restaurants for myself and others. Very little of the house is as I dream it could be. One of the first things that I made a priority before moving into the house was removing portions of the ceilings and walls in every room to install fixtures and computerized dimmable lighting systems. In the living room, the ceiling is sixteen feet high and composed of beautiful antique woods. I refinished and oiled the ceilings, added recessed lighting and duplicated the wood around the fixtures to make it appear as if the lighting had always been there. The living room is scheduled for sixteen different lighting scenes, my bedroom has eight, and the dining room has six. All of the rooms have excellent lighting for the art, combined with other light sources to give a warm attractive glow to the room. I experimented with this Lytemode system and then incorporated it on a grander scale at my restaurants. I'm a technoholic when it comes to light systems and fixtures—it's a total obsession. I agonize over the details of lighting design. It's certainly a by-product from my days of theater lighting.

Cameron's room was the only space I've spent concentrated effort on "finishing." I was so compulsive about it,

top left

As a child, I longed for beautiful clothes, magical palaces, bouquets of roses.... Today, my design studio in my home opens to a garden of nearly four hundred rose bushes; the majority over forty-five years old and priceless in their beauty and in the joy they give me.

top right

Six years ago I purchased a large traditional English Tudor home, for this architecture is the one that most closely fit my childhood perception of what a house should look like. Ironically, I have decorated almost all of the interior with contemporary furniture and art—but not all! The vase is by Anna Silver, my friend and one of America's foremost contemporary ceramic artists.

that I looked down at my tummy and told him he would have to wait a bit—his room was not quite ready (he waited a full two weeks, my most understanding client!) Most people enter my home and feel that many rooms are whole and complete, but revisions abound in my head. In fact for a full two years, only the large David Hockney print over the fireplace and the enormous Navajo rug occupied the living room. There were no chairs, no couches, but it made sense—we were never home. This room is now extremely colorful, in fact, it virtually vibrates with color and people never seemed cautious about striking up lively and often controversial conversations. The room is definitely not for the weak of heart, and when recently interviewed about what colors go together and which don't, I found myself responding that God never seemed to consider such a silly question when he produced a field of wild flowers.

Considering I am married to a celebrated chef, one might wonder why the kitchen and dining areas are not more elaborate than they are. Actually in the home that we owned prior to this one, this was the first consideration and I designed a wonderfully warm and fanciful performance kitchen with a dining area that opened to the living room as well. No expense or detail was spared in terms of equipment or finishes. If I win

the lottery in the near future, I intend to do a similar culinary extravaganza in this home: wood-burning pizza oven, built in woks, custom tiles…oh well, dream on. Actually, we do so much entertaining in the restaurants that, on those rare opportunities when we do entertain at home, we tend to do it quite casually by setting up a long table amongst the roses and other flowers in the garden. For the truly special holidays such as Thanksgiving or Christmas Eve/Channukah dinner, I remove all the furniture from the large living room and set up a long table for thirty-five or forty people which I decorate quite festively as I do the rest of the house.

Throughout my lifetime, seemingly unrelated elements have consciously and unconsciously inspired my work. My Neo-industrial concept for Eureka Restaurant and Brewery was founded on the overwhelming impact the movies *Metropolis* and *Modern Times* had on me. I primarily recall Charlie Chaplin standing in front of comically enormous moving gears and various mechanical parts. Eureka is my womanistic version of a cybernistic world. Chinois is my five-year-old fantasy of what I thought China would be like and I've often said "it doesn't…but who cares." Granita is my personalized three-dimensional metaphor for the sea. It is a complex combination of the wonders of what I

delighted in as I snorkeled in faraway waters, combined with the patterns of life I discovered under the microscope in the biology laboratory.

Design dictates so much of who we are and the quality of our life. As a scientist, I was constantly amazed at the natural order, mystery and power of life itself. As a designer, I take a multitude of elements and from chaos try to create a functioning system that incorporates beauty, harmony, excitement and a sense of joy and well-being. There are many talented people who dream about creating. But, imagination takes imagineering (hard work and tenacity) to make an idea a reality; as well as inspiration, passion for your craft, education, organization, communication skills and empirical knowledge, combined with integrity, commitment and a strong dose of "gumption." I feel my spaces are stimulating, whimsical and sometimes perhaps a little shocking. I've never been satisfied with "the status quo"; in all aspects of life the difference between good and great is in the details. I'm slightly unpredictable, irreverent and a bit flamboyant. Why wouldn't my home and work be as well!

This is my "dining room." Well, anyway, it doubles as Cameron's playroom and a place in which I can enjoyably write and illustrate my children's books.

Photography by Martin Cohen

Photography by Martin Cohen

Photography by Martin Cohen

opposite

The "vibrating living room" is filled with an eclectic mix of contemporary furniture and two Queen-Anne inspired chairs that belonged to my mother that I lacquered black and reupholstered in an avant-garde visual-pun on Chinese calligraphy. On the piano is part of my extensive collection of artisan designed frames custom made for specific photographs. Also, I am presently inlaying the fireplace mantel with crystals, geodes and stones very much the way I did at Granita restaurant. As I am busy building five restaurants at the moment, I imagine the mantel will be an ongoing process.

top

As one enters my home, this black-and-white foyer is directly in view—and then, one sees the electric-colored living room! I adore the vast contrast.

bottom

Morning light pours into our breakfast room awakening Irving, our parrot.

Photography by Martin Cohen

Photography by Martin Cohen

Cameron's bedroom is a backdrop of black-and-white checkerboard with painted Holstein window frames. The white oak floor is inlaid with an alternating pattern of ebony squares. All the custom fabric is done in a combination of black, white and primary colors. I photographed our animal family and had an artist hand paint their images onto fabric which was then appliquéd onto all the bedding, seating areas and throw pillows.

top

My late friend Eugene Jardin's six-foot-high by eight-foot-long sculpture, a combination of zebra-aardvark-and his dalmatian, dominates this part of the living room. Her name is *Felicity,* and she is joined by a German Expressionist canvas, two vases by Anna Silver, an Iguana bowl from New Mexico, chairs by Harry, our small *Dancing Table,* and a low cocktail table which I custom designed.

bottom

My son's bathroom was based on tiles we made and hand cut to resemble the patterns in Navajo eye-dazzler rugs. I first utilized this design motif in a small restaurant I designed called Shane. I adored the effect it had on everyone who experienced the color and optical illusion of movement the arrangement of geometrics produced.

Photography by Martin Cohen

Barbara Lazaroff ● at home 49

James Wines

at work

Photography by Andreas Sterzing

A wash of white stain frosts everything, even the wooden floors.

The SITE office is sort of where I live—maybe more a first home than a second one. I have a kitchen there and some sleeping arrangements. I lead such a nomadic life these days because all of SITE's work is abroad; so, I often only go home to watch TV.

Since our office environment at SITE is creative and accommodating, I'm not that eager to leave at the end of the day. For one thing, our firm is in the only Louis Sullivan building in New York. I consider him to be one of the true titans of architecture and this structure on Bleecker Street is a particularly beautiful example, with ornate Sullivan capitals on all of the twenty one columns in the space.

I was born in Oak Park, Illinois and, therefore, always held memories of Sullivan's work wherever I lived. I like the way he articulated space and provided ample light from all sides and his perfect sense of scale. In renovating the space in the Bayard Building, SITE tried to honor these elements. We wanted to retain an open environment which we feel is essential for the creative interaction of a collaborative group of artists and architects. It is designed; but it is also very casual and allows our team unlimited hanging surfaces for artifacts, notes, memos, and works of art. There is also plenty of floor space for models of projects.

Since the space was occupied by a factory until 1983, it had been partially destroyed; so, as a result, we took great care to restore the original plaster walls, ceiling, and sculpted column capitals. We made the eight-foot-high division walls in the Sullivan tradition (he generally used wood paneling) with metal egg and dart cornices and classical bases, but the vertical wall materials were wire lath over exposed metal studs. The entire space, including the floors, were then stained a monochrome white to suggest a "ghosted" image of the past. These lath walls—providing a succession of semi-transparent scrims throughout the interior—maintain the industrial intentions of the building. This context suits our firm very well, particularly as SITE is interdisciplinary and needs a feeling of flexible options.

Often offices are designed to be so slick and efficient that, for my sensibility, they really hamper creativity. I don't approve of a superimposed program for function. The purpose at SITE is not so much involved with style and form as it is with a desire to respond to every member of our group and allow for individuality. The space is a unified, but casual, matrix for idiosyncracy.

In the 1950s and '60s I lived in Rome, Italy, where I worked as a sculptor. It was my interest in architecture as a public art (so typical of Rome) that eventually led to my conviction that a building and its context should be seen as a unified kind of sculpture. This idea of a fusion of art, architecture, and environment became the basis of SITE, established in 1970. The objective has continued to the present; so I still think of a building as a filtering zone for information from its surroundings. So, it is logical that my own office is designed as an integration of past and present. I think the semi-transparency of the walls has worked especially well, because everyone working there can see each other and feel connected to a communal environment. The walls act as territorial membranes, rather than opaque barriers.

Over-designed spaces oppress inhabitants. It's as simple as that. Design can have a profound psychological effect to help or hurt people's daily lives. That's the reason I don't want to work in a space that makes you feel that if you move an ashtray you have offended the aesthetic. People in the SITE office can leave piles of work materials on their desks, pin notes on their walls, and it still feels right. In fact, these scrim walls seem to beg for the invasion of ever-changing elements. They are built of inexpensive industrial materials that have been used as much for function as for appearance; so, the space has infinite utility without imposing

some ritualized notion of performance on people. This sense of choice is important to me because what the world needs least is more monumental design statements. To me, livable spaces should be careful environmental interventions that respond to our new age of information and ecology. These forces determine the ideas, imagery, and uses of buildings in the future. If we neglect these important responses to nature, all other social and political concerns will pale to insignificance, simply because there won't be any people to address these issues. It seems to me that architects and designers have a moral obligation to use the environment wisely, encourage human interaction, and provide true "quality of life."

On the other hand, I don't believe the arts should be used to preach and declare. I prefer (as most people do) to make discoveries on my own and not have to face overt propaganda. Still, architecture can function as an example of environmental responsibility, as a monitor of social values. I don't consider it morally negligent if a client doesn't use solar panels, especially if they would be nothing more than intrusive and ugly technology tacked onto a building. But I do feel that architects should translate energy conservation into such appealing aesthetic results that clients want to be part of ecological awareness.

We are in a time of radically changing priorities in architecture. This century began with technology and industry as inspirational forces for design. Architects felt compelled to replace the superficial motivations of the Beaux Arts style with the spartan iconography of the Machine Age. But now, in the age of ecology, we are searching for a new imagery. Unfortunately, most architects are still committed to the traditions of Modernism and Constructivism and they don't want to ever let go. There is a clinging-to-security attitude. On the other hand, there are also a lot of younger designers very concerned with the environment and are using this dedication as a theme in their architecture.

One cannot save the world with the arts, but one can influence behavior with their messages. The green movement in architecture has begun to have considerable effect toward change. SITE feels part of this incentive. For example, we have just completed Ross's Landing Waterfront Park in Chattanooga, Tennessee. The whole concept is based on regional topography and life on the river and involves a major public space, gardens, and small buildings for services connected to the Tennessee Aquarium. It is focused on people interaction and they certainly seem to be responding. It opened at exactly the time of the Los Angeles Riots over the King case—when many cities suffered urban violence—but at Ross's Landing we enjoyed a peaceful and spontaneous mix of all ethnic groups that same day. I truly believe that the reflection of nature and ecumenicism of the park's design intentions was really

communicated and was responsible for much of the reason for this success.

In certain U.S. cities hostility has built up to such a degree that almost anything built by the controlling elite is perceived by the disenfranchised as being enemy territory. Yet, I think it is hard to attack a tree or a stream of water. Those massive formalist abstractions by architects, those imposing ego trips for architects, are much resented by the public. Most designers were trained in school to build this kind of structure; but, now, economically, sociologically, and environmentally, this direction is obscene. I spend a lot of time in Europe. Each time I return to the U.S., I am stunned by the sheer mass of built oppression in this country.

Returning to the subject of this space SITE did for its own purposes: I think it is anything but oppressive. I am always reminded of Louis Sullivan's compassion and how he was so in touch with his own time and infused this

honesty into everything he built. And yet, the messages of the space (prescribed for an earlier age) still inform us today. I think this is the true test of architecture—relevance at its inception and adaptive evolutionary possibilities ever after. SITE has tried to intervene at a point in this continuum and it has given our group much pleasure. Our space is always a work in process and that is why I find it satisfying to spend so many of my waking hours in this Sullivan created/SITE assisted ambience.

top

Twenty-one columns command attention throughout, their capitals ornamented by the building's architect, Louis Sullivan.

bottom

Current work by the designers is displayed along the semi-transparent partitions which are made of unplastered metal plastering lath.

SITE designers have made much of the furniture themselves. The rest is turn-of-the-century.

Stanley Tigerman and Margaret I. McCurry

at home

McCurry

As partners in the Chicago architectural firm of Tigerman McCurry, my husband and I are committed to the same goal: that of the creation of contemporary American architecture reflecting its own time. Yet, we work separately on individual projects as well as collaboratively on joint works, and both individually and together we bring to our work two different perspectives. My own approach to that goal has its roots in reinterpreting indigenous archetypal American forms. Stanley's method is to explore the disjunctive aspects of our society as he seeks to avoid dissimulation. Both of us have worked toward this goal through small projects, imbuing them with a symbolic content that some would say far exceeds their literal scale. And so it is with our own second home in southern Michigan harbor country.

With our house located on the main street of a small town, we were seeking a sense of order and tranquility...and also dream-making. In second homes, people tend to return to their childhood memories and reflections. They are more nostalgic. For me, though, this house grew out of a sense of the place it was in, and certainly the surrounding abundant nature was an influence. The tranquility of it all is something we both love to have in our lives.

top right

A half-circle boardwalk connects the car pad to the house. Thus our home's name is "Boardwalk."

bottom

The form is a baptistry or a silo, depending if one's reference is a church or a silo.

Tigerman

For the most part this house represents Margaret's efforts to find archetypal forms of rural America, Small Town U.S.A.

McCurry

It's a farm community. That's really the metaphor we were after. You can view the plan of the house as the community church basilica with the screened-in porch as the baptistry; or, the house can be seen as a barn and its clerestory windows as the barn's monitors. The round gazebo form at one side of the house is a screened-in porch, but it has the image of a corncrib and its industrial roof is the type one would actually use for a corncrib.

Inside, I was concerned with the efficient use of space. There are no corridors. Instead, one enters into a sort of piazza, with all areas communicating from the loft above to every room below. Every space is on an axial angle, so from every space one can look out to

nature. This type of perspective, with every area being on an axis with nature, is very prevalent in my work.

What this relates to in Stanley's work is more the zen of metaphor. In his work, moving backward and forward intellectually is what matters. The form that results relates more to his work than to mine, but the philosophical part of it is something we both share.

To me, it is important to be surrounded by good architecture wherever we live. In Chicago, we live in a Mies van der Rohe building quite happily, although we have had to make some adaptations according to our needs.

As a retreat, this second home is both tranquil and functional. It has a his-and-hers sleeping loft but there are drafting boards up there, too. So there is equal balance between the place we use as a retreat and a second workplace and as a place where we can situate people, in this case down below, and not be disturbed personally.

Tigerman

Of course, nostalgia deals with pain and grief and homesickness. The longing to go back is a sickness.

McCurry

But, it's not a sickness for us.

Tigerman

But metaphor creates a longing, because on one level you see the form of a church or a farm, whereas at a whole other level it is simply a weekend house. It is the metaphor that creates the nostalgia. If you see it as an industrial shed, then you see it for one thing. If you see it as an ecclesiastical precedent, then you see it as another thing; you're longing for your European roots. I'm just calling a spade a spade.

At the university, I'm currently conducting a studio class about nostalgia. When you're involved with metaphor it creates a longing and it's beyond oneself. It concerns a longing to return, something other than what one sees.

In this house we certainly were involved with metaphor, and that means transferring meaning from one thing to another. It's about something that's not there. A mixed metaphor.

In America, we have an architecture of exiles, an architecture about people from another place. The forms become hybridized. This hybridization deals with the fact that we're not from this place, we're from other places. So the fact is, we're all from other places and we're obviously involved, when we're involved, with metaphor. There are no original buildings in America, no original cathedrals.

Those who try to relate to a precedent here, like the Mission Style, or those who relate to the likes of Gehry or Morphosis, relate to the disjunction of society. The fact is that Frank Gehry, through using disjunction, is still using a metaphor that's sick in a way. He's responding to the same thing. He is still using a metaphor.

It is impossible to do anything which doesn't refer to another condition. So, these forms in this funny eight hundred-square-foot house which we did together is nostalgic on one level and, unfortunately, architecture is impossible to be other than metaphor. It always looks like something else. Even abstract art is still a metaphor, and it, too, is a sickness.

McCurry

For me the important thing is the comfort and where one can reflect freely. To wallow around in too much comfort one can't think about the future and always keeps too much in the past. I may have forms that are referential, and my clients are interested in that. And, I might reflect a Modernism, I have done that as well. But I am interested in American icons because I am interested in learning about the original spirits who created them and the aesthetic qualities of art and space and time. I don't think I really get into nostalgia in any derogatory form, because the work I design has a certain tautness to it that does not slip easily into a cute nostalgia. Actually, I am looking for a reductiveness of forms.

left

At the end of the boardwalk, a gazebo looks out over the pond beyond.

The main interior space is really a piazza, a room of double height and an infusion of light available from the clerestory windows. At the center, one can look through forty feet of the interior, providing almost an ecclesiastical feeling. The color palette reflects the nature beyond—the Michigan beaches and their soft white driftwood.

bottom

Simplicity has all the qualities of living in which we are interested. In our farmhouse second home, an example is our design of the sofa, repeating the grid that we used on the exterior and the sense of order that comes from a grid.

A silver screen and an industrial roof one would actually use on a corncrib form our sunporch with all its nostalgic overtones.

Howard Hirsch

at home

My home which I share with my wife, Elizabeth and some of our family.

As a designer of hotels involving a variety of functional activities, my focus in how I approach solutions deals primarily with two basic elements: space and good feelings.

Space is something to be sculpted, molded and internally carved out of masses of architecture depending on function such as great public spaces for ballrooms and smaller more intimate spaces such as lounges and restaurants. The organization and inter-relationships of these spaces create the synergism of a total design with each project having its own characteristics and identity. Identity will result from a combination of architecture and given themes. These given themes are a reflection of place, culture and frequently of a need to express a certain character such as background for an Italian or French dining experience.

I have been fortunate to work in many and various places around the world and always feel the need to involve myself with the locale I'm working in. This is reflected in the conspicuous use of art and well-crafted objects of whatever locale in which we are working. The diversity of cultures always stimulates and excites me. I often have the opportunity to research, find and then use the artistic skills of local craftsmen and artisans, as well as the wonderful, unusual antiques that can enhance and give more meaning to our work.

Creating good feelings is an essential part of my work, more than dealing with the correctness of the order of "good design." I would rather deal with intangible elements such as eye-delight, touch-feel, light and shadow, and warmth and comfort. I would both consciously and unconsciously use these elements in combinations to achieve a desired effect, which could be summed up as contrapuntally organized compositions that result in uplifting surprise and delight.

My background is more in art than in architecture and, as a result, my work involves the sculpture of space and the application of ornament through detail and color as though I were painting and sculpting at the same time.

I am not a very organized person. However, I am always in hopes that those around me will keep things together. I cannot tolerate overly organized and disciplined surroundings and will tend to put things askew if they are. Some people call it organized

chaos, some people call it charm. In any case, I like to be comfortable. My partner, Michael Bedner, is a compulsive organizer always cleaning and straightening things. I enjoy disrupting his compulsiveness to his chagrin. Somehow it works.

The Santa Monica, California, office of Hirsch/Bedner is more of a studio where creative work is being produced. Our work is much like a theatrical production with designers who are both script writers, directors and scenic designers, preparing a stage set for performers who are really hotel guests. The office environment is casual with skylights and trees which we find very conducive to the work we are involved in. The mood of the office is reflected in our own work schedule which is four-and-a-half day (but forty-hour) week. This provides a more intensive shorter work week and at the same time gives our staff more time for themselves and their families.

My own office is very friendly and casual. Some would say disorganized, but it reflects my own personality and the need to be stimulated by the objects around me. These include pleasant and

delightful art objects which I have collected, not to mention my modest fish tank faithfully attended by my secretary.

I believe my home which I share with my wife, Elizabeth, and three active dogs is a true reflection of my design philosophy. It is an environment that is light and airy with a great indoor-outdoor feeling and provides a lovely background for the variety of art objects that we acquired along the way. I am currently into Southeast Asian bells. The house is warm, friendly and inviting. We want our guests to be comfortable. We entertain a lot, giving dinner parties several times a month, and we have family on weekends. With four children, their spouses and three grandchildren, weekends are frequently very active.

In sum, my working and living environments are closely intertwined and I believe both reflect my own design philosophy which some would consider to be humanistic. I believe this would be a good descriptive word which is reflected in my personality and creative process.

Michael Bedner

at home

All photography by Jerome Adamstein

I'm emotional about design rather than philosophical. For me, feelings and emotions generate the energy and inspiration in a design. Evaluation, problem solving—all the steps in the design process—require freshness, energy and emotional commitment to the project. Becoming emotionally involved in the design is the only way I know how to work.

My needs are simple. I need the ocean, the sun, and I need the company of my children and good friends. It's finding the time to meet those needs that's complex. Let's put it this way: I work very hard to create a relaxed, informal, comfortable environment that allows all those concerned to shed their inhibitions.

In my office I need a large surface to work on. I have a five-foot by five-foot slab of marble I use as a desk. I need a well-organized environment that is not cluttered. That is probably the reason my desk always appears to be kept clean, while around me on the floor I am surrounded by stacks of paper and rolls of drawings.

An organized workplace is necessary for communication. Each of our five offices (Santa Monica, Atlanta, London, Hong Kong and Singapore) is designed to provide ease of communication between individuals, project teams, clients and representatives as well as among our offices. It does not have a high-powered corporate stance nor is it so structured that it becomes stifling. Even though we are a large group, we do not come across as being large, because we are organized into specialized teams to cover each of the different project types. This is the only way we can ensure expertise on a direct basis on each of our projects. We believe in personal service and want to keep the atmosphere as relaxed as possible. After all, if we cannot enjoy what we are doing and have fun in the process, how can we evoke emotion in our designs?

Our office is a large open space with high ceilings and skylights allowing natural light to flood in. Each of our offices has open studios encouraging an easy flow of communication among our teams. We work on an international basis and we hang flags from the ceiling for every country we are actively working in. We have clocks on the wall in the studio to see the times in our other offices.

Our libraries in each office are probably the most important areas. These are our resource nuclei. We have international sources and update collections for projects all over the world. Sharing resources between offices helps stimulate inspiration by always having on hand new materials.

Our conference rooms are kept neutral and clear as the presentation boards alone are enough to provide drama. The image that can be read upon entering our offices is open, light and fun with spaces filled with high-level activity.

So, my office is quintessentially "laid-back California," and my house is a beach house. At my house you'll find surfboards, friends, parties, even the occasional blues band or bout of Sumo wrestling in the sand. The office has flags and banners hanging from the ceiling, clients and friends dropping in, parties and even the occasional roller-skating Santa Claus. It's safe to say that my environments reflect the way I go about living and working. They reflect the emotional aspect of the designs we try to create. I hope the designs we create are fun; I hope they're productive, and I hope they're effective.

We got to be a big organization by always acting like a small organization. We want our clients to become part of the process. The same kind of "open house" policy I have at home I have at the office, too.

At my beach house, you'll find surfboards, parties, friends....

the Romanticists

James Northcutt
at work & at home

All photography by Mary E. Nichols Photography

I suppose one of the reasons I always expect so much in my home and work environments is that I grew up with parents who were both in design. While growing up, I spent a lot of time and gained early experience working in their beautiful Georgian design studio and furniture gallery in Longview, Texas. The building is now The Longview Art Museum, so it has maintained a lasting heritage.

My approach to design, as a whole, is to do projects that are varied, giving each one a strong sense of appropriateness for the individual client and to the locale. My hope is to create lasting design and to avoid design solutions that are trendy rather than timeless and enduring.

For my own environments, I like clean architectural backgrounds that become a good foil for a collection of items both antique and contemporary. I don't really have a specific collection, but I do enjoy art and accessories and enjoy collecting them. Therefore, I'm constantly editing, always trying to get back to the basics, unfortunately not always successfully.

Invariably, in my own home and office I have white as the background. In the past I have run the gamut of colors, including red rooms...chocolate brown rooms...but I have found that what I live in best is white. In addition, for my personal taste, I think art and accessories show off well against a clean background. Black is also important in any room; it gives a very necessary punch. Also, I try to work with scale in architecture and furnishings where I can achieve the sense of drama interiors need...sometimes overscaling objects in a small space to get the optimum impact.

I think perhaps one of the most important things is lighting. In the interiors I do both for clients and for myself, I have found lighting to be the major element which shows off interiors to their best advantage. It is key in highlighting art objects and accessories and creating mood.

In thinking of my philosophy of design and what it means to me in my own environment, I feel strongly that design and decoration are not just superficial. To be interested in design and decoration represents an appreciation of one's surroundings and, on a broad scale, even down to the objects one has decided to include on a daily basis. On a personal level it accounts for a style

that one has decided to experience in one's life. Design is an opportunity to express oneself and, in some people the ability to design is a gift to share with others.

Of course, one can also view that gift as a curse. The professional designer thinks nothing is ever good enough. There is always a certain degree of dissatisfaction, the feeling of trying to attain some ethereal goal you can never quite reach.

top

In the conference room at James Northcutt Associates, again the background is neutral. High ceilings and an extensive use of mirror provide a great sense of space. In the rear is an eighteenth-century cabinet from Sweden.

bottom

My office, located in the midst of the design market area in Los Angeles and also in a building which houses an antiques shop, is almost entirely white and black. As does my home, it provides a fine background for anything, most especially any project on which we might be working. The absence of color tends to present a dignified, business-like feeling and neutral foil for our projects.

This screen is probably one of my most favorite possessions. It is hand-painted leather and from seventeenth-century Spain, but it is so bold and dramatic it almost feels contemporary against the white background.

bottom

The large, tortoise-shell finished mirror above the fireplace in the master bedroom is an example of how furniture can almost become architecture. The overscale proportions of the mirror add drama and complement the simple design of the fireplace surround. Elements like that please me, as do black accents such as in the eighteenth-century Spanish religious painting in the background. I also like fireplaces in most rooms, and, when it is cool enough, you will always find them blazing.

I personally like blue and white porcelain because it is crisp and fresh, and a wonderful foil for other objects such as this stone Buddha. The black Chinoiserie table is a reproduction...mixing antique and contemporary furniture with good reproductions I find enjoyable and functional.

Carol Olten

at home

top left

With my Chow, Boots, in front of my Alice chimney.

bottom left

At my garden's end...The Lattice Cathedral.

bottom right

Jon-Patrick Butterworth and I, not Van Gogh, painted these sunflowers on the backyard fence.

I am a bohemian at heart, and most marble makes my feet cold right off. No wonder one of my greatest loves are those late bloomers of what we normally consider antiquity—the historic small bungalows of Southern California.

My own house sits on a corner in an older, unpretentious neighborhood in La Jolla. It has little to do with being grand, but everything to do with being special. The chimney has an *Alice in Wonderland* painting on the exterior, combining Alice with images of the Mad Hatter and the Cheshire Cat. There are giant Van Gogh sunflowers painted on my back fence with the artist's face inside the flowers.

The kitchen tiles feature a three-dimensional pink cat going around the backsplash and playing on a rope. In the office, where I conduct the affairs of my W. Rabbit Art and Design Studio, decoupage walls combine a myriad of images—my interpretation of silent movies in 2-D.

The rooms of my house have mostly old furniture. Some pieces have antique pedigrees, but not the majority. I have collected what has caught my eye, not my pocketbook—always feeling free to add an old French sofa here, an armoire with a carved gargoyle there. Clothing the furniture with hats, gloves, scarves and other wearable accessories also pleases me. The assemblages become like little theater sets slightly askew, as inspired by Magritte as they are by children's fantasy literature. Sometimes, children pass by my house and drop notes in the mail slot to Alice Wonderland. It figures.

My corner of the world has many unusual features. At the back of the house I have designed a gothic-inspired garden gazebo. It looks a little like a church, so we call it The Lattice Cathedral. Mystery, magic and illusion—how I like taking objects that seem one thing, then tweaking them to make them seem another.

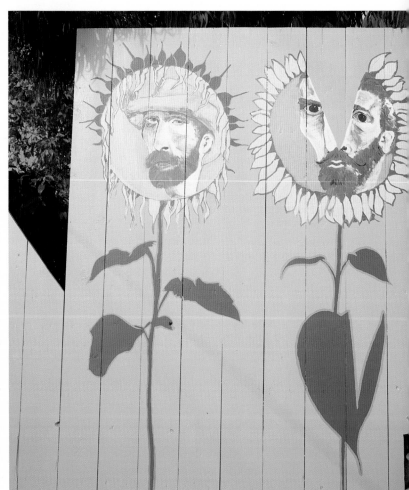

My generally eclectic
living room, with glove
collection, yellow guitars,
Tabriz rug...

All photography by Mary E. Nichols Photography

Irwin N. Stroll

at home

Interiors should be more than just something beautiful to look at. They should be inviting and functional, and the result should always be better than anyone initially envisioned.

In my home, I wanted to encircle my life with art, be it the art of architecture, or of lighting, or of my own art collection. I wanted dark backgrounds, since I deal with so many colors and so many different fabrics and clients each day, I need a retreat—a place that feels almost like a womb. The only drama I need is that which is played out before me by my art and my collections from my many travels.

When I was younger, I enjoyed viewing art either at a gallery or at a museum but as I matured and my clients matured, art became a very important design aspect of my work. I have always educated my clients and seen that, as they grow, their art direction grows, and vice versa. There is always a growth.

A home should not be a series of rooms filled with fabrics and furniture. It should have some form of emotional wrapping that keeps the whole package together. So when art or accessories are purchased they should represent some sort of emotional purchase, some sort of history. That is the reason I try to share what I've learned and what I know of the background of each piece I purchase for clients. If you just back up a van to a showroom and deliver the merchandise, there is only a monetary investment, not a personal one. Collecting is not about materialism, it enables you to capture certain moments of your life.

Collecting does not have to be an expensive endeavor. Sometimes the real treasures of the world are not monetarily valuable. An example is the time I went to Xian, China, and visited the unearthing of the terra cotta warriors. I was so overwhelmed by the intricacies of the excavation that I purchased, at a very nominal price, small copies of those warriors, and reinstalled them in a client's dining room as movable art on her table.

My mixtures in my home express the same spirit…David Hockney next to Xian statues…an antique Chinese chest that I purchased in a flea market along with a special Agam sculpture.

In my own home, I love my surroundings, filled as they are with memories of my collecting, of people, of places.

top left

As you travel and your eye develops, you become less dependent on others' judgments and predetermined monetary value. I have enjoyed very much this David Hockney, *Pembroke Studio Interior* (1984), especially because he once explained to me his approach to perspective and how he painted this work so that it seems to change depending from which angle it is viewed. Yet, I equally enjoy the replicas of the terra cotta warriors I brought home from Xian, China, and the emperor's chair I purchased in Shanghai… and I enjoy their juxtaposition.

top right

A dark and neutral background allows art, accessories and flowers to shine like stars at night.

bottom

How I enjoy placing antiquities next to contemporary art. The large painting is by Frank Stella, *Then Came the Butcher and Slew the Ox*, a multi-media work that combines lithograph, collage, woodcut, sculpture and watercolor— thus providing an education in techniques via one work of art.

The major design statement here is over the sofa, the David Hockney painting of *Celia with Clasped Hands*. The rest are from my travels—two green Murano glass horse sculptures purchased when I was in Venice, pillows fabricated from an obi I acquired in Japan....

Robert Frank McAlpine

at work & at home

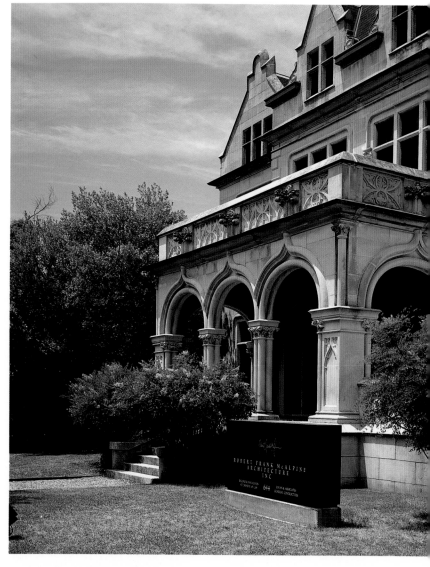

I like romantic environments and tend to never create a pure period anything. But, it is more complex than that. Generally, I think that all things have souls. Whether you know it or not, that is what you are attracted to and this is what "speaks" to the different parts of your personality.

Therefore, I never worry about staying true to period. I am simply interested in creating a wonderful camaraderie. However, I do insist on authenticity and authentic detail. If you are going to do a true French door, then it should exhibit all the delicacy and grace of a fine French window, not the awkwardness of the clunky substitutions that are so prevalent today.

In my home and office there is a mixed bag of things. By definition, I, as architect, interior designer and furniture designer, am pretty much a chameleon. A designer is a character actor. He doesn't play the role of a star. He doesn't develop an aesthetic philosophy and insist on it. Instead, I see myself pretty much as a problem solver, changing from one situation to the next.

My home and my office are located in Montgomery, Alabama. Both are in the original, older part of the city and within blocks of each other. But, whereas it was the building itself which drew me to establishing my office there, for my home it was the setting, even more than the house itself. It has a particular poise; it is removed from the street, and has a quiet, demure presence.

It is a Shingle-Style house with French and English influences. By nature, Shingle-Style is an eclectic mix which makes it inherently very casual, and the reason it is perceived more as a secondary, rather than primary, home. Common along the Eastern coast of the United States, this style exhibits the divergent traits of both town and country aesthetics, wherein the best of both meet. For example, in my own home there is the feeling of being on a small country estate, but also a sense of stature, similar to a Parisian townhouse.

The guiding force behind all my work is that, when designing something, even if it is new, you can design some soul into it. Everything has a particular, identifiable ego. For example, something may be demure, while something else may be self-important. Some elements of design are great company and accept the presence of other people

and other things, whereas others command the floor. I find with possessions as with people, those that make the loudest noise do not always have the most to say. Elements of design should be assembled as one might a dinner party, knowing it is not always the person who talks the most who says the most. And, I find design today is too often very loud and very empty.

Longevity is high in terms of my attitude when I create anything. Timelessness is the greatest achievement, and I think the greatest thing you can achieve in design is inheritability.

I primarily do architecture. I knew I was going to be an architect long before I knew what architecture was. I began to draw houses and do floorplans when I was five growing up in Louisiana; I designed my first house that was built when I was in the seventh grade. I started working for an architect when I was in the tenth grade. Stylistically, the houses I created then compared to those I create now differ greatly, but I have always made every effort to be "mature of hand" from conceptualization through final detailing.

Against this background, I have come to believe that the last good period of American architecture was the 1920s, when the picture postcard, American/European suburbs with great houses located near our great cities, were built. The only positive thing that

has occurred in our architecture in the last seventy years is Modernism. So, what I do in my work is reach back to a period, the latest being about 1920, and infuse it with Modernism to pull that period forward.

Furniture design carries with it a little less responsibility. Architecture I take more seriously because it affects more people than just the owners; it is public. Interiors sometimes can afford more eccentricity than architecture.

Basically, life is editing, and I edit with every aspect of my life. I think about architecture and design every waking moment. You can't get away from it. It is all around you. And, unless you take the time to shape your own environment, you may be affected in ways you don't want. I am a great believer in the behavioral approach to design. In other words, you can correct bad behavior and support good behavior by the way you design houses. For example, rooms sometimes have a tendency to become stilted, such as dining rooms. You can correct this by allowing the dining room to experience a flow of activity, with the result being a central gathering place that doesn't exude the pretense of a rare formal activity.

In the end, I find that elegance equals grace and grace has to do with use. The showrooms within a home that are not used cannot be beautiful. I

The French chateauesque style of my office is very rare in America, the most popular example being the Biltmore Estate in North Carolina, of which this, built in 1904, was a contemporary. It had been a private residence until I acquired it, and since we almost exclusively design houses, it provides a suitable and inspirational environment. The ambience is elegant, rich, sequenced and chambered, like a very beautiful home. It definitely influences the attitude of the five architects who work here. It is as important to work in a beautiful place as to live in one.

think that design in the next fifteen years is going to parallel design in the 1920s. Instead of enormous bullish houses, elegant but intimate and more modest houses are going to reappear as the type of places in which most people will want to live.

So, if the great houses of the 1920s came on the heels of Victorianism, then the houses of the 1990s and afterward will be a reaction to those very "High Victorian" houses of the 1980s. They were so pretentious and brash that they are uninheritable and will become used goods with no second audience. People want things that are real and that are more mature, not just for show.

top

In our Receiving Hall, there is a mix of things I have designed and classics by Modern architects. The giant white sofa by me combats the scale of the space, its high back enabling people to be silhouetted against a less complicated backdrop. The Grand Comfort chairs in black are by Le Corbusier, the coffee table by Mies Van der Rohe. In the foreground is my elliptical Walden Table, its shape being one of my favorites.

bottom left

My office on the old sun porch has French Empire doors of mahogany, as is everything else in this room. On the other side, the doors are ebonized oak to go with the rest of the house. The floors here are concrete and sisal.

bottom right

Our Conference Room was originally the home's dining room and is elliptical, a very coddling, warming kind of shape. The ellipse is special in that it allows two radius points, and here one is occupied by the conference table, the other the seating lounge area. Drop pendants mark both. The floor is inlaid with four different kinds of wood — mahogany, ebony, walnut and maple.

top left

The two-poster bed which I designed repeats the curve of the headboard in the foot posts, held in tension by vertical steel rods.

top right

I redesigned the fireplace, one of six in my home, to resemble a pier mirror.

bottom left

In front of my 1914 home in Montgomery's historic Garden District is the bench I designed and named after my mother, "Fannie Louise."

bottom right

The guest bath combines black tile, chrome fixtures and accessories with my custom Roman cross windows.

opposite

Architect/artist David Braly painted his impressions of gardens over my dining room walls. Old limestone surrounds the fireplace.

Imogen Taylor
at work & at home

I joined the firm of Sibyl Colefax and John Fowler in 1949, at a time when England was still recovering from the devastation and restriction of war. In many ways it was a perfect time to begin my career in the world of traditional decoration. There were still many shortages to overcome, but it was a time of reawakening. So many of the beautiful houses of England and Scotland were emerging from their wartime use as hospitals, officers' messes, children's schools and the many other purposes for which they had been commandeered. In addition, nothing had been done to them for ten years, and people's lifestyles, with the lack of servants and less help generally, were beginning to change.

As a junior member of the firm, I worked with John Fowler on many wonderful houses and thus learnt my trade in all its complex details. He was a hard taskmaster but a good, if exasperated, teacher. I learnt about periods of architecture and furniture. I learnt about colour in all its wonderful forms— in painting and fabrics. In particular, I learnt about scale and form and a way of living, using comfort and common sense as prerogatives. It could not have been a better beginning to what has proved to be a very long career in this all-absorbing world of decoration and design.

I have been lucky enough to work the whole of these forty-three years in a beautiful eighteenth-century building in the heart of London, with its own charming garden. It is rather like working in one of my client's houses, surrounded by antique furniture in human-sized rooms and in a family atmosphere. I think my clients enjoy the environment as much as I do, and it is very conducive to the sort of work we do together.

My office is in what would have been a bedroom in the eighteenth and nineteenth centuries and is prettily lined with very simple paneling and retains its original fireplace. The magnificent Yellow Room, which has become so well-known because Mrs. Nancy Lancaster decorated and lived in it for many years, is now a showroom for our antiques. This room always causes a gasp whenever someone sees it for the first time, as it is very unexpected, being an addition by Jeffry Wyattville in 1823 in the form of a ballroom to the eighteenth-century house. He used it to interview his grand clients when he was working on such projects as Windsor Castle and Chatsworth. The historic and traditional details of this house on Brook Street have been an unconscious influence in my life and work and I have certainly enjoyed this building as a second home.

My own background consists of a flat in Chelsea overlooking a square, in an 1870 building, with tall rooms and large sunny windows. Despite being in central London, it has views over trees and a balcony, all of which I enjoy. My country house in Kent, inherited from my parents, is my real home. It is there that I spend as much time as possible in a busy life and garden and grow plants in my greenhouse.

This house is a small, late eighteenth-century vicarage in the middle of a village with views over the Weald of Kent. The back part of the house is much earlier and has been added to over the past two centuries. The front is brick and the back is off-white weatherboarding and Kent peg tiles. The rooms are cottage-like but in the eighteenth-century part retain many of their original features and have a doll's house quality. My love of the country, country life, country food, gardens, flowers and animals is fulfilled in this house. It is there that I return to recoup my strength after my work which takes me as far afield as New York, Florida, Chicago, the Bahamas and many other places.

right

The exterior of Colefax & Fowler at 39 Brook Street London.

top left

Looking into the garden at Brook Street.

top right

A corner of one of the showrooms at Brook Street.

bottom

The Yellow Room at Brook Street, 1992.

top

A view of my house in Kent from the hill behind, showing the village.

bottom

The garden and fish pond.

top left

The front door.

top right

The garden.

bottom left

A corner of the garden.

bottom right

The greenhouse.

Allison Holland
at home

All photography by David Livingston

I collect colors for the interiors I design as I collect flowers for the rooms in my home—constantly. My profession and my life are so totally intertwined that it is impossible to separate them—and I would not want to if I could. One contributes to the other continually.

My firm, Creative Decorating, began in 1963 after my third child was born, making a total of three children in diapers. That situation alone was enough to foster an alternate activity. I started out on a small scale—handpainting and refinishing furniture—and the business grew slowly and carefully.

For two years my partner and I located our office in a tiny storefront shop in central Honolulu. It was complete with playpen in the back room, for there were now seven children between us. Then came a move with my husband to Maui, and at that time I made the conscious decision to further my career and become a professional member of the American Society of Interior Designers.

Up to that point, I had no formal training in interior design other than in brief seminars and correspondence courses. I also had an extensive library. Upon passing the exam given by the National Council for Interior Design Qualification, I gained the confidence necessary to expand my business. When we returned to Honolulu soon after, I opened my own shop independently.

Further advancing my education and training, I went to Paris with Parsons for six weeks to study French decorative arts and architecture. During the next four years, I fulfilled all fantasies of being a "store lady" selling antiques and accessories. Then I decided to move my drafting table and samples home where I could concentrate and focus on some major projects, including several in England and France as well as in many states on the mainland.

So, home is where I have been working since 1973, privately and quietly with one assistant. The studio here is stuffed with samples, catalogs and picture files from everywhere. Yet, as I sit at my full desk, I have classical operas playing on the sound system, a view overlooking Honolulu and the Pacific, and I find peace. Working in this way, out of my home, puts me in the creative mood necessary for formulating and enhancing projects and determining their aesthetic and practical solutions.

Perhaps the reason working at home has proved so beneficial to me is that my design philosophy is very much a part of my lifestyle. I believe that every environment can be improved and made more beautiful and that it is important to surround oneself with beauty. For me, that belief has encouraged me to extend my abilities in the areas of gardening, landscape design and flower arranging.

Extensive travel has been another source of design inspiration for me. I become totally absorbed with the images gleaned in foreign lands—from the ancient carved doorways in India, to the varied and clustered steeples in Austria, to the patterns of giraffes and zebras appearing at the same time and place for my camera in Kenya!

Between humanity with its contributions and nature with all its idiosyncracies, there is always something beautiful to witness and appreciate. My work is greatly influenced by this constant observation—and the longer I work in this profession the more I learn to see. Obvious expressions of this in my design are the use of antiques from many periods, objects from many countries, and myriad colors and flowers. Just like my home...just like my home office.

top left

top left

Because gorgeous porcelains are another weakness of mine, I enjoy using them in the traditional way. Flowers historically have always been used as porcelain's painted decoration, and I enjoy expanding on that with table linens, chair seats, wallcoverings…as well as my floral arrangement itself.

top right

In the living room, my more formal arrangements fit right in with the faux-finished green walls, the eighteenth-century Aubusson rug hanging as tapestry, the tiger velvet, the seventeenth-century wooden French madonna. Pin lights in the ceiling illuminate the flowers as well as the room's more prominent features.

bottom

My baskets filled with fresh blooms soon find their way into our conservatory-kitchen, where I am able to spread them out along my deep maple counter under dappled sunshine.

Photography by Tim Jenkins

Photography by Fritz von der Schulenburg

Photography by Fritz von der Schulenburg

Tessa Kennedy
at work & at home

top left

With my actor son Cary Elwes in front of our pavilion/poolhouse at Runnymede.

top right

The Gothic pavilion centered between the pool and tennis court is where we spend our summer days.

bottom right

Seventeen acres of garden surround my Victorian neo-Tudor home, Runnymede House, built on the site of a Tudor manor where the Magna Carta was signed.

opposite

Prominent in the hall at Runnymede is my daughter Milica's Palladian dollhouse. I made everything in it myself including needle-pointing the chairs and dressing the dolls in clothes identical to those my children wore when young, even kilts of Kennedy tartan. I am mad for miniatures and subscribe to several magazines on the subject.

There was a wonderful exhibition of British artists and poets at the New York Public Library not long ago, to which I took my children. In the exhibition was a poem by William Wordsworth about a tree in Windsor Park which is very near our house and a contemporary painting of the same tree by another artist of the same period. We knew the tree well. It is over six hundred years old and has a huge hole up the center in which the children and the squirrels used to adore playing.

When my family moved to Runny-mede and its surrounding seventeen acres in the early 1970s, I delighted in its large decorative chimney pots and huge mock beams. But I was rather horrified otherwise, for the twenty bed-rooms had been divided into five flats with only two bathrooms to serve them all. I proceeded to change its north-facing, darkly painted, brown oxtail soup gloom with as much light as pos-sible. Soft, warm tones and pastel patterns gave the lift I wanted, while I managed to incorporate treasures from all over the world, wherever my travels had taken me.

Yet, the most important directive of the design was to reflect not so much a passion for things as for life, and the way in which my family and I wished to live. I have five children, (Cassian, Damian and Cary from my first mar-riage to Dominic Elwes and Dillon and Milica from my marriage with film producer Elliott Kastner), and we love entertaining large gatherings of family and friends, and their friends, on a reg-ular basis. For this reason alone, life has always been a dictate for the design that surrounds me, not the other way around. I do believe one's home should reflect not only very personal taste but be an oasis of calm, a retreat from the world, a place where however much you travel you should always long to return.

Three things have had an enormous influence on my life. The first five years were spent in America, a vast house on the Hudson River, which because of its location and atmosphere remind me of Runnymede. The house was decorated by Dorothy Draper and most of the woodwork was painted white and huge cabbage roses covered the sofas and windows. The second part of my child-hood was spent in the Highlands of Scotland, baronial castles and masses of tartan. At the age of sixteen I converted to Catholicism and was again influenced by the beautiful architecture of the Gothic churches. The spirit of these influences has effused not only my homes but my office as well.

My staff of nine and I have spent the last six years in an environment that I truly long to get to every morning, as soon as I awaken. When I was looking for office space in London I was hoping to find an abandoned church to convert. Finally, I found an old studio/warehouse and proceeded to Gothicise it. Building a loft, I bought old altar rails to con-struct the balcony and three huge pairs of church doors. Additionally, I had a pair made to match and created two huge floor-to-ceiling bookcases. It is in those bookcases that I keep all our resource information and all the maga-zines, which I'm afraid we tear apart quite a bit, for we are constantly find-ing things we like and wanting to file them separately for easy reference. Those bookcases really contain a good professional design library now. When-ever we're looking for anything, we can always find it somewhere between A and Z. But to me, the best aspect is that we find it behind the visual poetry of those awesome, huge, and spiritually supportive old church doors.

Photography by David Montgomery

Photography by Fritz von der Schulenberg

Photography by Fritz von der Schulenberg

opposite at work

I converted four pairs of church doors into two huge bookcases which contain our sourcing library. At one end I created a balcony in the spirit of a choir loft, using an altar for the balustrade. Gothic style pelmets transform the square windows. Other storage space is hidden behind the fabric-covered wall.

top

The light and airy feeling at the other end of my bedroom, which I have tried to bring throughout Runnymede House.

center

At night when the lamps are on, the tracery of my magnificently carved Victorian four poster bed covers the ceiling with a profusion of patterns. In the morning the sun streams through the windows. Lying in my bed is like lying in state.

bottom

In my drawing room at Runnymede the whole of the ceiling is ornate plaster. Underneath, I combine pattern upon pattern, then allow the eye to rest a bit in between.

Photography by Tim Jenkins

Trisha Wilson
at home

I like to be in cowboy boots one minute, black-tie the next. My home reflects that, and my office does, too. So does my work. For the four hotels we completed at Eurodisney, we designed one Santa Fe, one Frank Lloyd Wright Sequoia, one cowboys and Indians, and one wilderness camp site. Unlike other design firms, Wilson & Associates doesn't have a "look"...and I am proud of that.

Yet, I do like a lot of openness and spaciousness. I love people and designed my home for entertaining, with an atrium and lots of indoor-outdoor areas so my guest list can go on and on. People say my house is really comfortable, and I think that's a great compliment, because we designers can sometimes try to be so perfect that comfort is overlooked.

I love flowers and surround myself with them all the time, in the office as well as at home. I also collect things from my travels, and since I have a global business and travel constantly, I never stop collecting. Whenever I walk past something I've acquired it brings back memories...of Africa, Singapore, London.... My style is eclectic and I guess my personality is too... unpredictable. I just like to go on adventures and have a good time. I love passionately what I do, and people tease me because wherever I am I say that is where I want to spend the rest of my life.

So my house reflects that...it's comfortable and unstructured in some areas, in others it's as formal as Versailles. But nowhere is it a place my friends can't relax. My friends are my family, and I want them to feel welcome.

It is a challenge taking care of so much yet traveling as much as I do, but it isn't a burden. My house is spotless even with my two big dogs in residence. I have two people working there fulltime and I am totally, extremely organized. I upgrade my collections frequently and clean out constantly. And, I'm always rearranging those collections. Recently, in fact, I found that I had so many little items that I started putting them together as brooches, and pretty soon I had too many of those, so now they're selling in New York.

I've always loved a lot of totally unrelated things...Shakespeare, bird watching, trout fishing. You can learn a lot by studying interior design, but you can learn just as much from the colors in a trout. I look, observe everything, and then talk about it to whomever I'm with whether they're interested or not. I guess I get by with a little bit of knowledge, and a whole lot of feeling.

top left

Basically, my house is a square with the atrium right in the middle, so the view of it influences almost every room. When I purchased the property, the atrium existed but not the planting. I wanted the lush feeling of a New Orleans courtyard, so I added a fountain that I found in France, as well as two eighteenth-century French urns which you cannot see here. At night the illumination by Craig Roberts, who designed the lighting throughout the house, is magical.

top right & opposite

Through my travels I have collected bits and pieces from all over the world, and one day I started putting them together with semi-precious stones. Today they are available as brooches at various stores in Dallas and New York City.

bottom

In every other room I have contemporary art, but in the dining room I have every wall filled with Old English, mostly nineteenth-century, dog paintings. The four here are by George Armfeld. The choice of a round table would be mine a thousand times over because it allows each guest to converse with everyone else.

Photography by Robert Miller

Photography by Robert Miller

Photography courtesy of Trisha Wilson

top

In my living room there is evidence of several of my evolving collections. The David Hockney print over the sofa and the Christo painting over the Italian console pay homage to my interest in contemporary paintings and prints. The various vases and boxes reflect my love of sterling. The stone eggs on the console reflect my un-ending fascination with the enormous variety one can find in this world…jasper and malachite from Africa, amber from Mexico, rubies in the rough from Russia….

All photography except where noted by Peter Vitale

Noel Jeffrey
at work & at home

Photography by Bard Martin

My home in New York City is a personal statement, but it is not one I have always had. When I studied in the 1960s at Pratt Institute, the emphasis was on the Bauhaus, with everything plain, white, tubular steel and leather furniture. The catch phrase then was Le Corbusier's "less is more." Yet, I also always loved classical architecture and the late eighteenth century, primarily French. So, I always had these two very divergent influences in my work, the cold and plain combined with that which is heavily detailed and opulent.

When I first went into business in 1969, I remained primarily involved with modern design for some twelve years. Minimal sleek design was popular. I used no antiques whatsoever. Instead, I designed almost everything, from the interior architecture to the furniture. I became well known for doing that particular type of work.

But as the 1980s progressed, the popular attitude toward design changed and traditional design became more important. So, since I loved it anyway, I elected to do that, too. When I designed this apartment for my wife Lynn and our son, I started to do traditional design mixed with modern.

I've always felt that, wherever one looks in an interior, one's eyes should be able to light on something beautiful. This style at which I've arrived does that for me. I find flowers among antiques next to some contemporary and classic items comforting. To be surrounded by things one has collected or designed over the years is a pleasure. I have a wonderful library of reference books on design, art, architecture and furniture; its placement among my possessions has been carefully thought out. I have always felt it extremely important that one's environment be an accumulation of one's experiences.

When I designed my office, my philosophy was somewhat similar but somewhat different as well. Pragmat-

ically, I wanted to create an office in which clients could see the kind of work we do, which is primarily residential. For example, there are mouldings everywhere to show the variety we could execute. There are various finishes from ceiling to ceiling, different wall treatments, various cabinetry of varying quality, and examples of decorative painting from faux bois on some doors to marbleizing elsewhere.

The office is a bit more eclectic than any one of my interiors, but the overriding theme is the same...and also my philosophy, that it is important to be surrounded by good design. I feel that the people who work here are always designing very luxurious and well-planned settings. They should also be in such a setting themselves.

top right

The Neo-classic feeling continues into the studio.

bottom

At Noel Jeffrey Inc. the overall feeling is again Neo-classic, but much more eclectic because we want to show clients various techniques and types of furniture. They can see the excellent cabinetry work of the mahogany doors I designed, faux limestone on the walls, marbleizing above the doors. I also designed the reception desk, sofa and table of satinwood and maccasar ebony. We also like to combine antiques with reproductions—such as the eighteenth century altar piece on the left and the reproduction open back Russian chair and the reproduction Louis XVI chair. Clients are often surprised to see how well made some reproductions are.

top

We kept my office neutral, because we use it for presentations as well. Again I combined Traditional and Modern— a Louis XVI desk and a Georgian chair are juxtaposed with a table I designed.

bottom left

The conference table is another example of my own design. The walls are upholstered for presentations, as well as photography of our firm's own work.

bottom right

The two baths provided an ideal way to show the two aspects of our work in a nutshell. The one on the right is Bauhaus in feeling. Designed to accommodate the handicapped, its sink is higher than today's norm, there are railings all around, and the door is wider. As we all know, form that follows function can lead to the best design, and we certainly have learned that universally accessible design can be beautiful.

opposite

The most important thing when one comes into a foyer is a feeling of excitement. Fortunately, the foyer in this apartment is large enough to hold the Steinway my wife inherited from her grandmother. The rest expresses my eclectic interests—the eighteenth-century French Aubusson tapestry, Louis XVI lyre-back chairs, the signed 1925 Sabino chandelier. The three glass doors can be mostly left closed day-to-day, then opened completely for large gatherings. It's a great way to manipulate the space. The ceiling mouldings, all marbleized, are of my design.

top

This living room truly expresses my eclectic approach to design. The draperies, though simplified, are almost Victorian in feeling. In the foreground is a Louis XVI bergere, and the rope bench on the other side is also Louis XVI. The large cabinet on the right is Biedermeier, another period I love. It is interesting in that it, too, is Neo-classic in a way.

center

We frequently have eight guests for dinner here, or I remove this table and have three smaller ones to accommodate eighteen. Again, our collection is eclectic—Biedermeier chairs, 1920s art posters with the one on the right by Jean Dupas, a Louis XV clock, Louis XVI wall sconces, and an early nineteenth century Italian sculpture.

bottom

Any writing I do at home is at this 1920s desk by Jacques-Emile Ruhlmann. The desk itself is of macassar ebony, the drawer pulls are sterling, and the keyhole is ivory. The mural was done by artist Dennis Abbe and it wraps all the way around the wall to the dining room beyond. It depicts the judgment of Paris, on the left, who is shown with Pallas Athene on the right, and Eros at the bottom left. It is sup-posed to represent our family. Obviously, we never allow ourselves to become bored.

Sig Bergamin
at work & at home

I think that design, especially when it is achieved in a person's home, is a direct reflection of his or her lifestyle. A person's home should inspire and motivate the inhabitant in daily life. Each client is an individual with different tastes, interests and hobbies, and this is what I try to make evident in my work; this becomes the important factor in the end result.

Combining all elements in a comfortable setting has always been my goal. I work in many styles and periods to best express the individual personality of a client and to enrich his or her life. I carry this philosophy through in my own personal environments.

They are many. My office in Brazil is located in the São Paulo neighborhood of Pinheiros, in a two-story house on Rua Cônego Eugênio Leite. I have an apartment nearby, and also a house in Camburi on São Paulo's northern coast. Then, I have an office in a townhouse in New York, a showroom, and apartments there and in Miami as well. Throughout all of them, I suppose, is a reflection of me—a longing for calm. (I stopped eating red meat long ago, and have tried to minimize parties and appearances in social columns as well.) Despite the eclecticism of my possessions, I aim overall not for excitement, but for peace. I love art, colorful art, and want to promote the exuberance of Brazilian artists, of which there are many fine ones. But, I mainly strive to surround myself with an intelligent collection that will create harmony as a whole.

My office in São Paulo offers peace simply in terms of its space—eight hundred square meters—and its immense amount of natural light. The limited palette of white leather sofas and easy chairs paired with a minimalist painting by Burle Marx also suggests mental calm. Two black leather chairs in front of a marble wall (that hides a small wash basin) offer no disruption, and a mango tree in this "winter garden" enhances the spell. At least I hope so.

Perhaps in my apartment in São Paulo it is easier to see my taste for the eclectic—but still the intent is to achieve a sense of calm, coziness and warmth along with intellectual stimulation. I have a great passion for art books and I am researching eternally, drawing from them much inspiration, not just for knowledge of the objects themselves, but also for intuitive stimulation. They are an integral part of that

My office in São Paulo is quite spacious—lots of white, plenty of natural light, clean lines, and just a few pieces of furniture. The approach is more minimal than in my home, as I need a plainer backdrop against which to discuss clients' dreams. In this converted industrial building, I have introduced steel columns, beams and open-web joists to accentuate the thirty-foot ceiling. The openness of the space, the floor-to-ceiling glass block walls and the clear glass panels emphasize the lush surrounding garden. A second-story mezzanine provides private administrative and production areas. The overall style is minimalist, and for me it brings to the atmosphere a sense of freedom and cleanliness with which I feel most comfortable.

for which I strive—exciting scenes manipulated toward balance and synthesis. If you study my design, that which appears to be an abandoned eclecticism in reality, is not. Although I may place a Victorian chair next to African drums (used here as a coffee table), I have actually been quite selective, always choosing those things which are classics of their own time, or else completely unpretentious possessions reflecting

memories of another culture more than some stylistic triumph. In my own way, this is an avenue to rid myself of materialism and concentrate more on people, on what's happening, and on what, in the end, is more important. I want to be daring, but I want to be unpretentious, too. I want to dispense with definitions.

All photography by Tuca Reinés

bottom

My apartment in São Paulo is located in an old building with high ceilings and well-dimensioned spaces. With its colorful and amply-sized works of art, it could feel like an art gallery, but the addition of antiques juxtaposed with contemporary furniture makes the ambience cozy.

All photography by Mary E. Nichols Photography

Erika Brunson
at work & at home

I have always been surrounded with art and antiques, even in East Prussia before my family fled to West Berlin during the Second World War. Decoration and design have been my passion, so I find locating fine works of art for knowledgeable and interested clients, manufacturing my line of antique reproductions, as well as making clients' homes not only beautiful but really providing comfort and function, more pleasure than work. Even the demands of a rigorous schedule and the disciplined attitude required of a professional interior designer today are, in a sense, a joy.

It has also become a source for my philanthropic activities, as all profits made from the sale of Erika Brunson reproduction furniture and accessories are donated to environmental and animal rights organizations.

Yet, I actually came upon making this my profession by chance. I always had viewed my main career as wife and mother. When my daughter, Kim Devore (now a television newscaster), left for college in 1974, I began to actively pursue my interest in Arabian horse breeding. Consequently, I visited the Middle East to investigate bloodlines and write a series of articles for *The Arabian Horse World*.

During my stay in Riyadh, I met King Fahad's nephew, Prince Khalid, who later asked me to find him a home in Beverly Hills. After visiting our own home here, he said its combination of elegance with an easy, open feeling was just what he wanted. So, since I had done this home myself, I accepted the challenge. I designed his home, and since then have never stopped designing, including the interiors of eight Saudi Arabian palaces.

So, this home is what really launched me, and I believe it was received so favorably because it reflects my belief in good design. I truly care about every square inch of space, and am willing to invest energy and enthusiasm in my personal surroundings.

After my husband and I sold our former larger home, we built this one on a view lot in Beverly Hills. It has two bedroom suites and a large living room—just enough space to suit our present needs, and much better for us than rambling about in spaces that had ceased being used. We entertain some, but not a lot, due to our both having busy office and heavy travel schedules.

top left

My office in West Hollywood is in the old Charlie Chaplin theater, a little freestanding Spanish building. I divided one huge room into designer stations, library, reception and bookkeeping. In the back there is storage space for all sorts of things.

top right

To embellish dinner parties: a Louis XV ormolu and rock crystal chandelier from the Patino collection which I acquired at auction at Sotheby's; eighteenth century Chinese vases; tobacco leaf Chinese porcelain; and rock crystal candlesticks.

bottom

Greeting visitors to our home: a pair of kneeling eighteenth century Thai Buddhas and one of the same period and origin which is standing.

opposite

Centered before a comfortable upholstered piece is a Burmese gilt lacquered wood reclining Buddha, eighteenth century Mandalay period, looking rather comfortable himself. The pillows are covered with antique chausuble fabric, the sword an antique from India, the mural by Douglas Riseborough.

So, it functions, works and is enhanced by pieces I have purchased all over the world. But, perhaps its greatest asset is that I truly love these pieces. I know their history and have memories of where I found them. For myself as well as for my clients, I document everything and keep researching further, learning as much as I can about design, art, history and culture. In the end, the result is not just skin deep luxury but, ideally, an inspirational collection of some of the world's finest ideas expressed through line, form and material, executed by fine artists and craftspeople. That is why interior design is, and undoubtedly always will remain, my passion.

opposite

I am in constant touch with Sotheby's and Christie's and keep myself aware of other auctions of interest. Here in the foreground are a pair of Regency carved gilded beech armchairs, circa 1815, which I obtained from the Kalef Alaton sale. Beyond are a pair of Louis XV giltwood fauteuils a la reine, mid-eighteenth century, signed by Louis Poussiee which I also reproduce.

top

Here I satisfied my love of blue and white with a set of Kangxi blue and white dishes and yards and yards of blue and white fabric and wall-covering. It proved to be the ideal setting for my eighteenth century Chinese cabinet with its multitude of blue accents, as well as this painting by Professor Helwag.

center

My passion for rock crystal lamps is once again in evidence in the master bedroom. Here they are nineteenth century French, and sit atop two early Georgian gilt gesso side tables. The early George III carved giltwood pier mirror I acquired from the estate of Michael Taylor. The portrait of Catherine the Great was painted by Anna Rosina Mathieu in 1880.

bottom left

Looking through the Louis XV carved pine doors: a painting by Modigliani. On this side: a bronze cat by Giacometti.

bottom right

My very eclectic taste leads me to placing in proximity works from vastly different periods and places, antiques and also reproductions. Here in our living room I have included: a Régence ormolu-mounted ebony bureau *plat*, early eighteenth century; a painted wood Bodhisattva; an eighteenth century ormolu and malachite duckbill gueridon table; a Regency armchair I purchased at the Kalef Alaton auction and which I now reproduce.

Vicente Wolf

at work & at home

top

My TV tower is
permanently tuned
to snow.

bottom

The conference room at
my office enables clients
to see one of the things
I do best—integrate
antiques into a con-
temporary space.

The difference between my home and my office is that in the apartment, even if something's not perfect, it can stay there and I can play with it until I feel it's right. In my office, I won't have anything that's not working in the best possible way.

My apartment keeps changing constantly. It's already different since these pictures were taken. But, the office has a format that remains basically the same. Oh, chairs are recovered, works of art change, and accessories are rotated. Things I buy in Europe are displayed about the space. Yet, it's a place of business, so you must keep that in mind.

Your office is the one and only place where you can truly put across to a prospective client your point of view as it pertains to business and your approach to business, as well as your style of design. So, it's very important that it speaks to what your sensibility is. Still, in many respects and not surprisingly,

my office is similar to my home, especially in the conference room. With the photographs not hung but leaning on a ledge and a blend of period objects and different points of view, it shows how I can deal even with the most traditional art and accessories and still come across in a fresh, clean way.

My home changes much, much more. I keep seeing it in different ways so I'm always trying to make it look different. Most laymen want a space to be set, but I'm always moving things around or recovering the upholstery. And, I'm always trying to keep myself excited about the space. I want to never stop evolving, so my home has to constantly evolve too. I have neutral floors and walls now...but for a while I had everything blue...then black. It's white now because I live in a loft space and that is a situation you approach differently. To maintain its integrity you can't have colored walls; but, I am about to change the floor. I'm going to

make it like a country road with trompe l'oeil dirt and leaves made to appear three dimensional. Then we'll cover it with lacquer and small globs of cement. Finally, I'll place plants around in garden-like areas.

The point is that you have to change. Fifteen years ago I was doing karate chop pillows, but now I purposefully make them limp with just half the filling so they don't look like Chiclets.

Once a week I take a room and readjust it, and that's different than maintaining it. When a room is just maintained, it dies. But, if you change the fabric or get a new painting, it breathes new life. People don't allow their clothes to look as if they are caught in a time warp. They should treat their own surroundings with the same respect.

The light-colored table by Jean-Michel Frank and the figurine left to me by my grandfather are constants in the space, but are moved around.

I don't want to stop evolving, and I don't want my home to get caught in a time warp. This Aubusson was once on my floor, now it is a tablecloth. Examples on view from my photography collection are always different, or if not different juxtaposed with something else, creating some new idea that will start me off changing things again.

top

My favorite chair—which I waited almost two decades for until it became available at a close-out sale—and Robert Mapplethorpe's *Poppy*.

center

I get rid of possessions almost as quickly as I acquire others, in this case the bowls from Turkey and a gateleg table.

bottom

I like chairs, obviously. One hangs on a free-standing wall in my kitchen.

Richard Himmel

at home

I have no design philosophy. Anybody who does winds up in a corner that he can't get out of, whereas I can change my style to suit the personality of every client. So, I very particularly do not have a design philosophy, and if it were otherwise I would have broken it long ago.

I let my eye and heart guide me. It's kind of boy meets object. I read a great deal and study and travel and look at furniture a great deal. I've been to all sixteen Biennales des Editeurs de la Decoration in Paris, and because I have no design philosophy there's nothing I'm not open to.

Even in my own home in Chicago and in this second home in Palm Beach, Florida, I didn't start out with a particular plan. I'm not self-conscious about how I get ideas...I'm just grateful when they come. But, I am a compulsive buyer and a compulsive collector, so everything in the home I *had* to have.

The problem is: being a designer makes nothing ever seem exactly right. What a pain in the neck that is. It makes my life very hard. Nothing is ever quite good enough.

My work environment is different. I can design in the back seat of my car, and my seventeen books...eighteen really but the publisher didn't want my Western...I wrote wherever I happened to be. So, I don't know how important design is really in terms of making you productive. On the other hand, I certainly believe design is more than skin deep...goes all the way down to the innards or, if there is a soul, to the soul. Other than the people who are vital to my life, design is the whole thing. It was neck and neck with bridge for awhile, but design came out on top.

Despite my continuing involvement with our showrooms which are ideal depositories for the accumulations resulting from my acquisitive nature, 'it's the *assemblage* that still turns me on.

That's the reason I've always thought that William Pahlmann and Billy Baldwin were worthy of emulation. They knew how to put all those things together.

Of course, I have my baseball heros, too...Gabby Harnett, Rogers Hornsby...I still want to be Ryne Sandburg when I grow up. He plays second base for the Cubs, makes seven million dollars a year, and he's worth every nickel of it.

top right

The painting over the Japanese lacquer figure is by Fernand Léger.

bottom

These chairs are fiberglass replicas from a mold I had cast of a Louis Philippe papier-mâché creation I found in France. It was inlaid with mother-of-pearl and what not. These I had hand painted to match the fabric on the cushions and table skirt. The two figures are seventeenth-century French.

top

Over the years I have collected this nineteenth-century Burmese furniture from the Colonial British period. It's not that easy to find, but when you do it's usually in England where the British would bring it after they returned home. The upper painting is by Marino Marini who always does the man on a horse. Underneath is a work from Adolph Gottlieb's *Burst* series.

bottom

These Anglo-Indian chairs were carved during the turn-of-the-century during the period when the English would go to India, then want some local craftsman to try his hand at Chippendale. They were originally a yucky brown. I added the red lacquer.

The dark green of these faience busts, the color a particular factory in Apt in the south of France makes everything, and set me going on the green-and-white color scheme. These figures represent the four seasons as do those of coral stone in the living room. The collage is by Conrad Marca-Relli. The chest underneath is from Arles where Van Gogh painted so much.

bottom

Our living room has mostly museum quality eighteenth-century furniture, which I think mixes well with a little French Art Deco, but most is signed and is really of exceptional quality. However, I think we've done it so it doesn't look like a museum. It looks contemporary and comfortable.

opposite

The faience over the fireplace was made by an unknown ceramicist from Ballauris.

Lynn Wilson
at work & at home

Photography by Regine Turmel

Lynn Wilson Associates International offices is located in La Palma, a three-story Mediterranean-style landmark hotel built in 1924 in Coral Gables, Florida. Its courtyard is built around a fountain and fully-grown mahogany trees. We completely gutted and restored its twenty-four thousand square feet of space, and restored its barrel tile roof and French doors. Our office and studios take up almost ten thousand square feet of its three wings.

opposite

In our loggia is an 1856 rosewood grand piano, the third Steinway produced in the United States. My father was a concert pianist, a composer and orchestra leader so it is very dear to me. The two jade masks, one lying on the piano and the other on a stand, are from Mexico. The painting is one of a pair placed on either side of the fireplace. They were completed in 1703 by an Italian court painter for the Palace of Versailles. The vertical piece is a three-part eighteenth-century carved bishop's screen with a velvet and gold tapestry insert.

In a sense, I believe that artistic people have been placed on Earth to preserve beauty and joy, and in the hospitality market the opportunity to do that has become extensive. Lynn Wilson Associates deals exclusively with the design of hotels, golf resorts and historic restorations. We have seen design become a truly global market. Whether for business or personal pleasure, so many people are traveling to exotic destinations that one might think of the hotels where they stay as being the perpetuators of culture for humanity. The quality of design established at these hotels is truly setting the standard for the quality of taste those same people might reflect in their own environments at home. So, as designers, we carry quite a responsibility.

I myself have traveled a great deal all my life. For the past twenty years as an interior designer, I have been doing design projects in Europe and Eastern Europe, South America, Japan and throughout the Pacific Rim. In addition to my univeriity architecture and design studios, I received a masters of arts degree in art history. It is inevitable that wherever I go I collect art objects and place them in my own homes, one of which is in Miami Beach and in our offices in Coral Gables, Paris and Los Angeles. They mean so much to me in terms of memories, and in terms of appreciation for the people who made them that they seem less like objects of art and more like friends.

My environment has become a scrapbook of travel memories so, even though the effect is very eclectic, I feel it all works. The collections reflect the spirit of each of the artists represented in his or her work. The artisan who made each piece, be it an Aubusson carpet or a Regency bergere chair, would have spent a large percentage of his or her life reflecting culture and beauty in a way that could be passed on from generation to generation. These pieces have soul, so it is right that they not be abused or discarded, but instead be cherished and loved and passed on to others who will appreciate them. These nameless artisans live on through these treasures and perpetuate beauty and its ability to inspire further creativity. Creativity does need to be inspired and perpetuated.

Not surprisingly, some of my favorite design projects involve historic preservation, which deserves a lot of support from those of us in the design

community. If we were concerned only about projects' economic viability, then historic preservation would be a lost cause, because it is less expensive to tear down and rebuild from scratch than to preserve. But what does that cost us in terms of the forests we demolish, in terms of the hillsides we are gouging to turn stone into concrete? Saving history also means preserving the environment. As professionals, we'd better start doing our part in communicating the message of preserving our environment.

Wherever my husband and I are, either together or separately, we take time to involve ourselves in local culture and history. We are archaeologists, in fact, and have done three documentaries, two for BBC and one for ABC. In one we flew a hot air balloon over the plains of Nazca in Peru, viewing the huge ground formations claimed to have been produced by the ancients to worship the Sun God. We built our balloons in the style depicted on ancient pottery we had found. Another of these

documentaries showed my husband Bill and me journeying to the original home of the Queen of Sheba in Yemen. The surrounding desert had been a city of three hundred fifty thousand inhabitants who had developed incredible technology in creating a huge dam, thereby converting the surrounding desert into magnificent gardens. Today that technology is completely lost. The people became lazy, they lost their knowledge and interest in preservation. They repaired the dam poorly and incorrectly until it finally eroded and ceased functioning. My point is: if you don't preserve history you lose both the present and the future.

I feel that we designers are among those who, as disciples of beauty and joy, have the responsibility to preserve that which already exists as well as to produce more. It is that philosophy which is behind what you see in my own environment.

opposite

The courtyard of our Italianate Mediterranean villa is completely enclosed, with the protective colonnade providing shelter for more antiques and my wood carvings from Bali.

top

To the left in this view of our living room is a French Régènce door surround that I made into a fireplace. Other pieces I treasure here are an Aubusson carpet I purchased in England, two gilded Baroque columns from a church in Italy, and a part of our impressive collection of pre-Columbian artifacts.

bottom

One of our homes is on the water on Miami Beach. This former Hoover Estate built in 1932 by the developer of the Hoover Vacuum. In the dining room, the floor is cut coral, so I selected the table base for the harmonious color of its carved stone double dolphins. The ceiling is a native wood, cypress. I have had it pickled to again be in harmony with the other textures and finishes here. I chose a muted palette to create a soft background thus allowing the antiques to be featured: Italian angels, brass can-delabra, a French chandelier, and an Addison Mizner carved chest beneath a painting from the school of Sir Thomas Lely, the court painter to Charles II. Lely had an entourage of four painters and this work, which I particularly admire, was painted by a woman artist.

Jacques Grange
at home

top

With the self-portrait of
one of my favorite artists,
Christian Berard.

bottom

Detail, private office.

Before I moved here, my flat in Paris belonged to the writer Colette. To live in it now provides a great opportunity.

It doesn't look exactly the same as when she lived here, but I have respected the spirit of the place she left behind, its sense of unmistakable harmony and protection. The feeling that this was a good time in her life lingers still, and you can almost see her husband sheltering her here. So I have redecorated, making compositions everywhere of my own collections, but everything I have done has been inspired by the Neo-classic style prevalent at the end of the eighteenth century, the style of the architecture in which she lived.

It is a style that seems extremely beautiful in this particular situation, for my flat itself was built in the eighteenth century and it overlooks the garden of the Palais Royal. My windows open to the gardens on one side, the street on the other, so that special Parisian half-light filters through, influencing everything as if almost subduing it. There is not one bronze, one shell, one painting, one thread of fabric that is not touched and changed by it.

In response, I have washed the walls the color of stone and chosen a brown and gold floor covering that seems to speak about the trees in the garden. Even the curtains in the salon are the color of the building's grey-blue roof tiles. And every hue is just a tint, just a suggestion, as it would be so wrong to have full-blown vibrant color in this atmosphere.

In honor of the spirit of Colette and because I too love books, I made sure that immediately on entering my home you would see volumes upon volumes, continuing from the salon to my office and even lining the passage to the dining room.

My private office here, unlike my office on the Rue du Faubourg Saint-Honoré where the atmosphere is more that of a studio, is more cozy still with even more collections...and more books. I remember Coco Chanel's flat and all those books on their sides as if they were sleeping. Not mine. I really use my books. I place them like books. I love walls where you can see nothing but books. For me they are the supreme reference of work and culture.

In the dining room I allowed myself to be much more colorful, more exotic and almost Oriental. The thought of

good food and stimulating conversation allows one to project a more vivid tone in this room, despite the pre-existing skylight that brings in that softening Parisian light here as well. Still one wants a dining room to be prepared for as much gaiety and exuberance as might possibly grace a meal in one's home.

By my designing in response to the mood of each particular room in this flat, you might say that I am writing my own type of literature, my own script. In fact, every item that I have chosen to have around me tells a story. Nothing is here just for decoration. Every item I have is mine because I love the artist who made it or the memories it holds for me. Each and every piece has a story behind it and, at least for me, fills the atmosphere with mood and drama and, throughout, with thoughts of Colette.

In my bedroom, I have located the desk in the exact place where Colette wrote her novels. The bed too is in the exact position where hers was. She lived here happily for the last fifteen years of her life, and the vibrations are good.

top

In my salon, everything has been inspired by the Neo-classic style prevalent at the end of the eighteenth century.

bottom

My dining room is more exuberant, always ready for a party.

Detail, salon.

top right

In this view toward the Palais Royal, the light of Paris makes everything seem transparent.

bottom left

A trio of my favorite things...a Biedermeier chair, two nineteenth century French lamps, and a mirror by Jean-Michel Frank.

bottom right

My bed is placed precisely where Colette's was.

Louis Shuster

at work

bottom

French doors, skylights, windows—all were added when we renovated this two thousand five hundred square foot houseboat and converted it from a residential configuration to an office including a conference room, full kitchen and complete design library.

opposite

Outside my office, the deck provided a much appreciated ambience for meetings and informal presentations.

Until August 24, 1992, Shuster Design Associates was operated from a plush, twenty five hundred square-foot houseboat moored at Marina Bay in Fort Lauderdale, Florida. It was the most tranquil yet stimulating work environment I had ever seen, and I never would have left it if it hadn't been for Hurricane Andrew.

I am originally from Philadelphia and had never lived anywhere near water. When I moved to Florida in 1980, I naturally fell in love with the weather, the scenery, the lush landscape. I said right then and there my office had to be on the water. Next, I had to locate the proper houseboat for my needs, and

this was difficult because houseboats aren't that plentiful and most of the ones that do exist are just boxes on a barge. I wanted something much more architecturally unique, something I could really sink my teeth into.

I employed a gal who specialized in houseboat sales, and we flew all over that state, from Tampa to Key West. We finally found one moored at the Diplomat Hotel in Hallandale, Florida. It was fifteen years old and built by Surfside Six, probably the best houseboat builder in the country. Why, they guaranteed the hull of the boat for one hundred years. It took five-and-a-half days to tug her from Hallandale to Ft.

Lauderdale, and I had to change her from a three-and-a-half bath residential structure to an open office space for some seven employees, but it was the best decision I ever made.

The boat was extremely dark, so we enlarged all the windows and put in two eight-foot skylights. We installed a new staircase to the second floor, providing a much cleaner line than the existing one. To add drama to that structure, we installed a two-story piece of plate glass extending above and below that staircase.

The beauty of working on a structure like that is that there are no codes as to what you can and can't do—no electrical codes, no permits that have to be pulled—because it is not considered real property. For example, I probably could not have used glass in that way, had this office been on land.

The look I was after was light and white and clean, to exemplify the type of work we do and also to serve as a good backdrop for art. To show commercial clients how they could maximize smaller office space we installed two offices back-to-back, with a computer area and illuminating shelves in each, in a total space of nine-feet by twelve-feet.

We used a greater variety of materials than we might usually use in a space this size, because in our own office we like to show clients the abilities of our various suppliers. Still, I have a predominantly less-is-more approach to design so the overall look was still clean. It was in fact a twenty-four-hour-a-day showcase, because when people would come to a meeting here they would never want to leave. And, when prospective clients would come aboard, I wouldn't even have time to bring out my portfolio before they would be sold.

So, it was a great sales tool as well as a great personal pleasure. However, it all ended that day in August '92 when the hurricane-infuriated elements twisted her over on her side, sinking her until not one inch remained above water.

Nothing was salvageable, and I, of course, felt devastated—along with some thousands of other poor souls in Florida at that time. Since then, we have established beautiful offices a short distance away and have opened a showroom featuring accessories from Brazil. This time, however, both are on land.

opposite

Visitors are led past a contemporary reception area, down a short corridor, to a cutaway domed ceiling over a rotunda featuring a trompe l'oeil painted mural of classical architectural elements. The ceiling, fabricated of fiber-reinforced concrete, is a replica in section of the ceiling at the Pantheon in Rome. At the center of the mural is a view of a Renaissance Palladian villa containing a discrete logotype of our design firm. Trompe l'oeil columns frame doorways which open to corridors that lead to our offices.

top

In my own office I have designed the desk with a drawing board option. I no longer have to turn my back to the door every time I pick up my pencil.

center

Conference Room

bottom

A network of open beams borders each office area, imparting human-scale intimacy without cutting the designers off from the expansive spatial volumes.

the Classic Purists

Motoko Ishii

at home

Kamakura city is located about forty miles southwest of Tokyo metropolitan area, and it was the seat of the government during the Kamakura period (1192–1333). In this quiet city, there are many historical sites including famous temples and shrines.

Kamakura is a resort which is known for its beautiful Shonan beach. On clear days, one can enjoy the charming scenery of Ohshima and Enoshima islands, and Mt. Fuji. Geographically very conveniently located, Kamakura is about fifty minutes' train ride away from Tokyo. Coupled with the expressway, the advanced transportation system enables a large number of people to commute to the Tokyo area. In that sense, Kamakura for Tokyo people might be equivalent to Long Island for the people of New York.

My house is built among the mountains of Kamakura, where an ancient temple called *Gokurakuji* (once very big in scale) is located. The south side of the house faces the mountain slope, and we can hear birds singing and see squirrels playing.

My house is made up of two parts that are stylistically different. One is the traditional Japanese-style house which is almost one hundred years old; the other is the modern annex which was added five years ago, in 1987. The Japanese-style house has a formal entrance hall, three Japanese rooms, and a bathroom for guests. In this house, rooms are all done with Japanese traditional architectural mannerisms except for the bathroom. In the newly built annex, we have a dining room, a kitchen, a bathroom, a utility area, and a storage space on the first floor, and three bedrooms on the second floor.

These two types of architecture, the Japanese-style house and the modern annex, are connected by a half-octagonal-shaped living room which is decorated in Chinese taste. Pieces of furniture selected for this room are all antiques that are more than one hundred-fifty years old.

In front of the Japanese-style house, there is a Japanese garden where we can enjoy seasonal flowers such as azalea, cherry blossoms, and apricots that are planted on the south side.

The newly-built annex was designed by an architect and a professor at Tokyo University, Mr. Hisao Kohyama. I designed the lighting throughout. Japanese lighting fixtures were selected for the Japanese-style house, whereas fixtures from all over the world were chosen for the modern annex.

I like to spend my time in the *shoin*-style room with *tatami*, thick mats of rice straw finished with a cover of woven rushes. This room, in the Japanese-style house, is almost one hundred-years old and was made for the highly knowledgeable person who was the owner of the formal Japanese restaurant named Kohraku in Akasaka, Tokyo. Shoin rooms were not usually designed by architects, but were often ordered by clients who have a vast knowledge about architecture. Those clients would then usually give the detailed orders to the carpenters.

Sitting in this tatami room and making drawings for new ideas is my favorite way to spend my time in this house. In my daily life, I am very busy carrying out lighting designs that utilize the latest techniques, and this place provides an ideal atmosphere for my creative thinking. Also, the relaxation I get in this house prepares me for my busy life in Tokyo.

opposite

Traditional shoin-style room in Motoko Ishii's Japanese-style house.

top right

View of the house from the garden, with the Japanese-style house on the right, the newly built annex on the left.

All photography by Yoichi Yamazaki

The living and dining rooms of the newly-built annex, viewed from the corridor through the courtyard.

Massimo and Lella Vignelli

at work & at home

Massimo

The most important thing in our office is the certain spartan, serene approach We like to express our philosophy, and that is to say we're not interested in trendiness and things of that nature

Also important is the efficiency—like the conference room, with the light from above, with nothing present except for what will be in use at a particular meeting. And that's what I mean by serenity—not technical, not busy, not overdone.

To maintain a space like this, whether in the office or at home, is a matter of discipline. We never buy souvenirs and all the collectibles that hang around forever. When you buy something, it has a validity at that moment, but then its value to you is quickly consumed and it becomes a piece of trash hanging around.

We do have some things, but they're inside a cabinet and on the inside of that cabinet it's a tremendous mess. Outside it's soothing and clean. But when you want to remember the past, just open up the cabinet and there it is.

But to have such things outside cabinets doesn't enrich your life, they just make it more and more miserable.

There are people, of course, who like to collect, say, famous champagne bottles. That's all right. But I like to have nothing around myself. I see beauty in spatial proportions, not in accumulation. And this is why we do not accumulate possessions. We think we already have too many.

Let's say I enjoy the spareness, not the emptiness. Emptiness is a space devoid of interest, but a space that is interesting in its proportions is never empty.

The right proportion—there is a backlog of thousands of years of good exercise about it. There's this continuous search for purity and perfection through proportion. And scale—scale being proportion in relation to man, proportion being absolute beyond man.

Our color palette is limited in our environments both at home and at work. I don't treat this as a limitation, but I look at color as I look at everything else—in terms of necessity and appropriateness. If I need yellow I will use it. And if I design a restaurant, I will probably use peach. But in the office I would probably always use white. For colors, we like very much to get

them directly from the materials we use rather than from added pigments, at least when this is possible, because the color natural to the material is integral and has a truth. But there's no problem with adding color on the material—it just needs to be appropriate.

To convey a message of elegance without luxury—that's what we are after and what we like to have surround us. Because if you can achieve elegance with very poor materials, then you've really accomplished something.

Also, I like rooms to express the life lived there rather than to be decorated to pretend they have a certain life. So that is what you see in our home.

In the library we live a great deal, so it automatically gains its expression. Then we have the living room where we would like to stay during the day but we're never home, and it shows. It's more abstract there.

The bedroom was designed to be nice and clean, but it's always messy because all the magazines and things always pile up. But that's the nature of the room and that's all right.

I'm Italian, and I believe in the commedia dell'arte approach to things—the tradition of having a certain structure and then improvising within that structure. We're talking about design rather than theater, but it's quite similar. The basic house is there, but it has to be allowed to acquire a life of its own according to how people live there and how much they live there.

When I look, for example, at conventionally designed interiors, it seems they always stay the same except for the floral arrangement. Instead, I like interiors to be like good shoes—beautiful and comfortable and expressive.

We now have acquired a country house, a one hundred-year-old farmhouse. It has old American furniture, and we've left it very much as it was, trying not to do too much so as not to erase its "life." In that, it's Vignelli...but it's also our escape from Vignelli.

Lella

To a great extent, we live and work surrounded by our own design. Most of the furniture and objects in our home and studio we designed ourselves. So that is part of what sets the tone and standard for our own environments here in New York.

And as you can see by our design, we are really fighting for a lot of simplicity and minimalism. We are trying to come close to perfection in our own terms by subtracting, by eliminating as much as possible. Naturally, because we have had a long and busy life, objects pile up even if we don't want them—especially in the home. Even so, it is rather sparse.

However, our spaces do not lack sensible comfort. The furniture we design is created with comfort very much in mind. I don't think we have the problem of our spaces looking good but not being livable. In fact, I am quite opposed to that. On the other hand, when designing for ourselves we sometimes give up comfort. For example, the walls in Massimo's office are made of lead hand-rubbed with beeswax. We couldn't give this to a client...especially if designing a public space.

In my own office, we have used particle board for the paneling. It looks like limestone and we really like it but the door is big and the particle board heavy so the touch-latch doesn't work perfectly. We don't mind taking care of it, but a client might. Also, we did not seal the flooring and therefore must be careful of stains. Most clients would not want to deal with that.

Yet for clients it's much easier to decide if they really do want something innovative when they can see an example of it in use in our offices. And this makes it much easier for us to convince them, too.

Another particular aspect of our own office and home is the space. Our office is fifteen thousand square feet, and we were fortunate to find an apartment with a room that has double-height ceiling—New York probably has only a half-dozen buildings like this. Yet it is not so much a question of size or height that makes the real difference. It's more a question of proportion and the cut of a space. The size itself is not a necessity for a space to be beautiful.

Also important are the materials. I feel one of the most impressive aspects

of our office is the dry wall ceiling, which gives a completely different feeling than the institutional tile or exposed ducts one sees in so many offices.

In addition, we have very little art on the walls. We feel that art either should be created especially for a space, or should be so well chosen that it looks as if it had been. Also, art is not a trend or a fashion for us as it is for so many people who buy one moment and then sell the next.

Often, however, we have no art, We like to let a room speak for itself. For example, our conference room is very bare and monochromatic. But with the illumination coming from the skylight, the effect is beautiful. The whole attention is on the people at the table and on the drawings that eventually will be on the table.

top

Reception desk, Vignelli Associates.

bottom

Area of the 24-station studio.

top

Large Conference Room.

bottom left

Massimo Vignelli's own office.

bottom right

The Library.

Charles Jacobsen
at work & at home

top left

The nineteenth-century carved wooden figure in the background is from India. She represents Parvati, consort of Shiva.

top center

Water is a key element in my work. In the showrooms, for example, nineteenth century Japanese granite basins called *mizubachi* are placed facing the entry. Mizubachi were used in temples and the tea ceremony, as well as in Zen gardens.

top right

I see my work appealing to very few. Those I work with understand the sensitivity of interior space and its relation to garden space. This cohesion must exist, whether one chooses Japanese things or not.

center top left

My Los Angeles showroom is also my design office. The space works wonderfully as a meeting place and visual aid for clients.

center top right

The pair of nineteenth century Japanese bronze bud vases sit on a *wakasa nuri* lacquer table. The screen and table are of the same period.

center bottom

I sleep very simply. The futon sits on an antique Japanese *ajiro* mat. A six-panel gold leaf screen provides an architectural backdrop.

bottom

These handmade Japanese winter tea bowls are lined with silver and gold leaf.

I was born and raised in Honolulu. After secondary school on the island of Hawaii, I attended college at Hamilton College, Clinton, New York, and the Sorbonne in Paris. Immediately after receiving my degree I lived for two years in Kairouan, Tunisia, a very conservative inland city and pilgrimage center. I mention Tunisia as I believe it was there that I first began seeing what would later develop as my personal style and taste in both architecture and design: blind exteriors, limited decoration, rectilinear shapes, interior gardens, and rooms ringing interior courtyards. Sparse furnishings allowed the architecture to exert its power. In addition, I was captivated by the way Arab cities are formed by clusters of houses and neighborhoods, with confusing, winding streets, making arrival both personalized and special.

Although I have lived and traveled throughout Western Europe, it was only in parts of Spain, with its Moorish influence, that made similar impressions on me.

This attraction to Arab architecture and design was reinforced by five years spent around the Mediterranean and Middle East.

I moved to Chicago in 1973, and opened my first shop, China Clipper, in 1982, relocating to the Merchandise Mart in 1984. I expanded the operation to Los Angeles in 1991.

When I began traveling in Japan to buy inventory, there was, unconsciously, an awakening of a preferred architectural style in seeing traditional Japanese houses. Though far away in time and place from Arab architecture, everything about these houses spoke to me in the strongest and most natural way. I understood for myself why things were done as they were, and was pulled toward the best in the Japanese domestic building aesthetics.

I was to be similarly touched, after expanding my travels to India, by certain of that country's Mughal and British colonial architecture. The common threads would be beautiful forms, elegance of line, purity, edited simplicity, empty space, and importance of garden to structure.

I feel in reviewing my memories that what also drew me to these styles of building was their sense of oasis. I feel, in my work both in the showrooms and in the designs I work on, that this is what I best have to offer... oasis. It is more, obviously, than shelter: it is safety. It is also seclusion, privacy, and the limited but complete joy of nature's presence.

All that I see and choose is fed through this point of view. It makes choices and decisions quite easy for me, as there is always the overriding goal of creating oasis that guides me, giving great freedom at the same time to create in many styles. The guiding principal, however, is constant and uncompromised.

The wall hanging is a nineteenth-century Chinese bamboo undergarment, framed in gold leaf. It hangs above an eighteenth-century Chinese Luohan bed.

Arthur Gensler

at work

Photography by Toshi Yoshimi

W hen you enter the lobby of a Gensler office you see a very neutral but welcoming space. You won't see any of our projects in the reception area, and for a specific reason: we're not trying to sell a style. We don't want a visiting customer to have a preconceived idea of what he or she is going to get from Gensler. I just don't like that—influencing what our customers want for themselves.

So, we don't show our own work, but most of our offices do have changing exhibits by outside artists. We do this for a number of reasons: to enrich our own experience, to expose us to different artists and types of work, to lend a pleasing variety to our office environments. Our visitors enjoy the art.

In designing our offices, we want to convey the idea of professionalism. We are professionals, and our clients are experienced professionals who have successful businesses of one kind or another. We want to demonstrate that we, too, are successful at what we do and that we know how to use our budgeted funds to design offices that are functional, tasteful, and not overly opulent. We're not trying to play the starving architect who's a great designer, nor are we trying to make a specific style statement in the lobby. We do want to create a neutral lobby space so that clients or potential clients reach the presentation area without forming an opinion on design.

In fact, even our presentation areas are designed to be very neutral so that we can focus on the subject at hand. The colors and materials of the client's project, not our own offices, are the important items. Whether we're presenting a very traditional design, a contemporary design, or a unique approach, the room itself doesn't inhibit our presentation. We want to be able to work with any medium—videos, projected slides, or models—and have nothing interfere with presenting ideas to our clients.

In the same way, we don't want to overwhelm our clients with our reaction to some current issue. For example, our designers have put together an environmental manual which focuses our attention on many of the endangered species of woods. It's an important issue, but not one that has dramatically changed our design efforts. We are certainly more sensitive to energy conservation and to the woods that we use. But our philosophy is to

not get carried away with any one theme because we think that it all balances out when we address the main issue—to provide the best possible project and service to our clients.

I also think we sometimes get our clients too hung up on every little detail. They're not trained to make all these decisions. When you buy a car, someone doesn't show you every screw and every valve. Sometimes we architects and interior designers are too obsessed with showing our clients every detail and getting their approval of it.

We have become a global firm . . . with offices in New York, Washington, DC, Houston, Denver, Los Angeles, Irvine, San Francisco, London and Tokyo. We are experiencing different cultures and different attitudes and different ways of doing business. It fascinates me to see how we can work with them all, to meet the requirements of making our projects flow smoothly. Again, it gets down to trying to do the best possible job for the client, and trying to do that shapes the way you work.

As for my own home, it most certainly is not a showcase. I didn't do the architecture, so it is not a personal demonstration of my design philosophy. The furniture includes some nice pieces, but they're there to be used. We have four sons and now four granddaughters. And a dog. Our house is a great place because it's very lived in, comfortable and personable. We have many parties there and we love to play

Photography by Nick Merrick © Hedrich-Blessing

Photography by Toshi Yoshimi

sports. We have lots and lots of pictures of our family as well as paintings by some artists we like. The house sits on San Francisco Bay, so we all have a wonderful view. Our house is always filled with lots of people. My wife is very active in the community; she is always entertaining groups and keeps busy day and night. We have no lock on the door...people just come and go...it's wonderful. We never know who's going to be there, and that's fine. We have fun there. That's what's important to me, not looking at this or that detail, or showing any of my design talent.

Of course, there are people to whom that personal statement is important. But, my statement professionally is the body of work our firm has ac-

complished. At home, it's the people who surround me, the pictures of my family, my mom and dad.

But, I do like privacy. I don't have to hide, but I will sit and read on weekends, for seven or eight hours, then play golf and tennis, and then go out. Life has changed for us since our four boys went to college and started lives of their own. Now, my wife and I are alone, so life is a little quieter. I seldom take design work home or telephone associates and clients on weekends, as many architects do. My home is my home and that means privacy. I study and read and think, but I don't continue all my day-to-day work. I believe that if I sit an entire hour and get just one new idea, that hour was well spent.

With our having become a global firm, it is critical that we stay current. I don't have any hobbies other than my work. So, on weekends I go over everything I've collected during the week. I really fight to keep the pile of magazines from getting too high. I probably go through seven or eight publications every night as I sit and watch television. I copy the articles I want to read more thoroughly, and then usually read them on airplanes.

The computer has dramatically changed our work. I personally haven't gotten there yet. I deal with an enormous amount of computer-generated information, primarily because I deal with the financial and communications aspects as well as the design aspects of the firm. And, as most of this is computer-generated, I should really get myself up to speed technologically. I know many people who collect just the right data and wind up with a beautifully designed collection of research. But, I'm not into that. So I tear out and circulate certain pages of magazines, marking pages to be copied for certain people to read. People ask, "Why don't you just put all that on the computer?" but I don't know what I'm looking for...I'm just searching for new ideas.

So, that's why I'll have three hundred to four hundred pages of material I've collected on trips and why my files are so extensive—I've been collecting like this for fifty years! I devour the material, but I haven't yet begun to devour it via the computer. But I will.

I have learned to communicate via the fax. Just the other day I was talking to an organization about tying our entire firm together by video-conferencing, in order to get the whole firm together at one time at one place... which we've never been able to do before. Whether that can be done effectively or not I don't know. For example, every six weeks our Management Committee meets. Now, if we did all this on video-conferencing, we wouldn't hear all the side comments, all the exchanges that occur during breaks. I think video-conferencing is very public; it captures everything that happens in a meeting. But, it doesn't capture the side dialogue. And that side dialogue is important.

Another example is going to conferences and exhibits. I suppose we could accomplish the same thing from our desks, except we would miss the face-to-face dialogue, all the social interaction. That's what really motivates people: the chance to hear other people speak, to see for yourself how they've done something. I don't know what I'm looking for until I see it, so I can't ask someone to send it to me, or ask someone to go and report on something for me. I can spend a day at a market, see one hundred showrooms and find maybe three or four items that I think are good. I could never have someone else walk through those showrooms and get the same reaction I get by doing it myself. So, now they're talking about virtual reality—ways to further enhance the feeling of really being there...and, although I'm a great believer in technology, I just haven't had it inculcated in my facilities the way I probably should.

top

Denver, CO office
The reception area was to be accessible from both elevator and escalator, and, as a result, the plan follows a diagonal that bisects the floor. One side is dominated by the open studio plus a library, lunchroom, secretarial and word-processing areas. The other half, aside from the reception zone, comprises two enclosed vice presidential offices, two conference rooms that can be combined into a single room, plus offices for accounting and marketing. To emphasize the triangular shape of the reception area, a blue suspended ceiling mirrors the form of the terrazzo floor below. This blue plane also links the reception area to the conference rooms and is intersected by a red beam and portal, which carry across the diagonal to the studio.

Photography by Nick Merrick © Hedrich-Blessing

**Santa Monica
(Los Angeles), CA office**
The design goal was functional work spaces of pleasing scale and proportion, with some full-height walls to demarcate studio organization, and comfortable conference areas. Low walls separate work stations, while floor-to-ceiling walls conceal conduits and provide support for hanging displays. Every station can be adapted for either manual drafting or CADD by adding or removing a detachable drafting board; each is wired for access to the network.

Photography by Nick Merrick © Hedrich-Blessing

Photography by Nick Merrick © Hedrich-Blessing

top

New York, NY office
Our ability to service a growing number of clients on significant projects in the Eastern United States and London, England, has substantially increased because of the layout efficiencies of the planning concept in these new offices. The morale of our staff has been raised by the high level of the workplace environment. The spaces shown are the presentation room with view toward secretarial workstations, located as an important point of transaction. The palette used in the offices included anigre, (a light wood resembling oak), black leather, chrome, steel and neutral fabrics ranging from grey to beige. Underneath the internal stairway is a space for floral arrangements or furniture display.

left

Houston, TX office
The challenge was to achieve maximum effect with maximum reuse of existing furniture, while providing functional flexibility, within a strict budget. A Miesian aesthetic was chosen for its elegance and reserved contrast to the potent activitiy typical of this architectural firm. A central multiuse area consolidates mailroom, employee lunchroom, printing and office supplies, and library/ resource center. One final objective was resolved in the furniture program, which successfully blends the existing with the new. The result is a showcase of flexibility for the firm's clients.

Photography by Chas McGrath

Washington, DC office

The elevators open onto a large, graceful area. The main conference room, opposite the elevators, has three pairs of doors which, when opened, double the reception space, enabling the area to comfortably handle staff meetings as well as social events. The main conference room appears monolithic but is very functional. The A/V cabinet, projection screen, drapery pocket, light switch panel and storage closet are all hidden behind movable panels that have no visible hardware. There is a continuous chair rail which flips down to be a chart rail that accommodates presentation boards. Two sections also pull out to provide a credenza for luncheons. The wood and etched glass tripartite screens opposite the glass doors slide into hidden pockets to reveal the building windows, providing flexibility to the appearance of the room and hide the less attractive facade across the street.

Photography by Nancy Clendaniel

Scott Johnson
at home

Design is a continuum in my life. It is the thing I think and live. It is not something I start in the morning and put away at night when I go home.

Design has to do with attitudes and instincts. The longer you are involved with it, the more interesting an instrument you become, and your instinct becomes fact. Yet, you are constantly evolving, because you are developing attitudes all your life.

I myself am interested only in future-forward design, not derivative arts and architecture. However, I do use history as a springboard into the future. For example, since moving to Los Angeles, we have always chosen to live in Spanish revival homes of the 1920s and '30s. These homes built in the early days of movie-making were frequently designed, we suspect, by set designers. The quality of rooms is usually splendid and the stylistic elements of the houses are informed and adventuresome. The houses are also well-built and generous enough to survive all manner of intrusion and modification. Common are bare wood and tile floors, massive original plaster walls, hand-carved doors and ceilings and, with luck, traces of original hardware.

For me, just now, the house is a moving target. My architectural and design responsibilities with Johnson Fain and Pereira Associates keep me traveling, and I tend to work on projects at odd hours. My wife is on call as a physician and, with two small children, we have several live-in assistants. The design character of the home needs to support and survive all this.

Naturally, all the vitals of the house have been structurally made over: central kitchen, bathroom areas, and pantries. With only minor structural changes to the rest of the house, everything has been refinished and refurnished. In fact, this is an ongoing process. As we've always been extremely mobile, furniture requirements vary and I am always designing pieces which find their way into the house. Except for a consistent pursuit of balanced light, day and night, and a refinement of fixture detail, there is little in the house which needs to "work" with something else. Paintings, of course, are bought for interest, not location. All pieces come and go, and relocate frequently as we do. This probably gives the house a kind of back-lot quality, where we build sets, re-stage, and go on to the next picture.

top

When I undertake a project, I always ask myself what are the best examples of that sort of thing that have been done before. And I don't mean just the last fifty years but the last two to five thousand years. So I have a large library of some five thousand volumes on art and architecture, interior design and gardens.

right

Many of the paintings I collect, such as these by Lynn Lipetz, are architectonic in nature, and so is the little gaming table by Roy McMakin. I like the informality of the big fat wicker in these Donghia chairs, and the strength of the torchère from Barcelona.

opposite

Our dining room is fairly spare, but the crushed corduroy of the Donghia chairs is comfortable. We felt it an appropriate counterpoint to the Corbusier airplane table and the reductive painting by Fay Jones, *Ancestors at Sea*.

Photography by Mark Lohman

Photography by Mark Lohman

Perhaps one of the aspects I like most about residential design is that, since you live in such close proximity to it, you can appreciate the details. Here in my wife's dressing room, I have added small gold-leaf beading on the maple millwork. Also, I designed the mirror with a hand-rubbed mahogany frame set into bronze so that it can rotate three hundred and sixty degrees.

top left

I made this desk for my wife. It has an aluminum frame engaged around a radial set of drawers and is finished with brass knobs and a Makore facing, all of which has been quarter-matched. The chair is by Czech artist Boris Sipek.

top right

Everything in the master bath I designed anew—the mahogany millwork which was then fabricated by Jonathan Plaskett, the Venetino marble countertop, the Venetian glass tile. I designed everything, that is, except the English cast porcelain tub which I found at a secondhand shop, and the black and gold maquette by sculptor Beverly Pepper.

center left

The wonderful lines of this British army officer's chair make up for the fact that it's terribly uncomfortable.

center right

I suppose if I have one twentieth-century hero in interior and furniture design, it would be Jean-Michel Frank. He had an incredible intuition about scale and finish and the ability to render informality as elegance. So this table, which I based on one of his side tables and then asked Jonathan Plaskett to fabricate, is an exception to my not wanting to copy the past. I admired the original, and, since I could not have it, I made my own.

bottom left

Jonathan Plaskett made this table which I designed for the library. The legs are hand cut and inlaid with three colors of plastic laminate. The top is the white Venetino marble I admire for being extremely elegant yet neutral in color. It sits on a Joseph Hoffman carpet designed for the Palais Stoclet in Brussels.

bottom right

This is the Cadillac Table I designed in quarter-matched sycamore with bronze inlays, sort of cruciform bronze fins that pass through the table's center.

Sally Sirkin Lewis

at work & at home

When I enter a room, I would be uncomfortable were everyone to turn around. I would prefer to walk in quietly and be acknowledged accordingly. I feel the same about interior design; no one thing should jump out at you; rather, the space should simply envelop you graciously.

As an interior designer, and later, when I started designing furnishings and textiles for J. Robert Scott, this same sensibility invaded my consciousness. In the showroom designs I have created, I wanted nothing to fight with anything else; I intended for all furniture and textiles to coordinate and live well together as a cohesive environment, thus creating a sense of tranquil harmony throughout. As a dividend, we soon realized that our clients, by not being distracted with all sorts of colors and patterns, were better able to envision their own creative requirements for their clients.

Honestly, though, I do not design the showrooms this way simply because this neutral statement provides a good background for what it is we market. I design this way because it is what I personally love and require for my own working and living environment. My designs are an extension of myself and the way I see the world. If something is beautiful in its line and detail, it need not be embellished. To do so would be like wearing an elegant gown with beautiful lines and exquisite quality fabric, and then destroying it with overly decorative jewelry.

If I am fortunate to be working with wonderful architecture, I don't care to detract from, smother or contradict it. I am interested in imparting its sense of space, proportion and light. There is no need to overly adorn but rather to work within the core and enhance it. Good architecture stands on its own.

I believe I keep a very focused eye. When I design an interior, I approach it almost with the eye of a camera, or as a painter. My mother was a fine painter, and what she imparted to me carries over into my work. I like rooms to look like paintings...as I would have painted them and, in my own mind, already have. I see interiors as living landscapes. When I am shopping there may be all sorts of wonderful items around me, but I don't even see them. Sometimes, I store their images in the back of my mind for future consideration. I usually have previously visualized or sketched the details. For

top left

In my J. Robert Scott & Associates showroom, New York City.

top right

My New York showroom reads like another home I might have designed for myself. Here I have combined two murals by San Francisco artists Evans & Brown and Art Deco bronzes with J. Robert Scott furnishings designed by me.

example, when I was shopping in Paris for our New York showroom opening, I knew I wanted only Art Deco transparent crystal or art glass, ivory or black ceramic animals or figures, bronze Art Deco sculptures, and Empire Doré bronzes. I was so focused that I was able to shut out all the thousands of other beautiful objects around me.

My husband says that I go through life with blinders, not looking left or right—only forging straight ahead. He's probably correct. In addition to being so focused when I shop, I also do not visit other showrooms, so as to avoid mentally storing someone else's ideas. I don't ever care to imitate or copy—but prefer to create. As a designer, I feel it my obligation to do so.

On the other hand, we all draw from past periods and other cultures. We interpret and fine tune them for current lifestyles. My eyes and senses are open at all times to all things and to the world in general. We can gain inspiration from anything and everything. I can drive down a street in Los Angeles, or look at some architectural detail half way across the world, and even though I'm not consciously searching, I am absorbing...devouring. I look at a tree branch and in my mind I see the graceful curve on a piece of furniture. I see a dress of fabulous fabric and visualize an interpretation of it covering a piece of furniture. One day I was remembering the wonderful suits my mother wore in the '40s, and I decided to introduce a collection of hand woven pure silk boucles to our J. Robert Scott Textile line. Until then, this type of fabric had never

been used in home furnishings. But, as I was sketching some new upholstery designs, the boucle weave appeared in my consciousness as the perfect texture for these designs.

Yet, even though I am constantly designing or sketching new ideas (indeed I never stop thinking about design), I am rarely able to turn the meter off—I am constantly editing also. Our lives are so hectic in so many ways that I think we all need a sense of space and freedom. Paring down can rid our lives of some visual confusion, thereby affording us time to think and dream of new paths to travel. For myself, I couldn't live or function without visual tranquility. Clutter literally clutters and confuses my mind and even seems to affect my equilibrium. I guess that's why I enjoy editing so much. In my own home, as well as in the showrooms, I attempt to achieve a sense of balance, symmetry and space even though the trade-off is eliminating product.

Symmetry, balance and space are priorities for any of my environments, as they bring a sense of order to things. For example, when we moved into our Los Angeles home, I first placed the art in the living room. It was almost dusk when I completed the installation and with the soft light and shadows dappling across the bare floor, I remember thinking how beautifully elegant and peaceful it looked without any furniture. Wouldn't it be wonderful, I thought, if I didn't need to be conventional, and could simply put two beautiful Régence chairs in the middle of the room, with nothing else to dis-

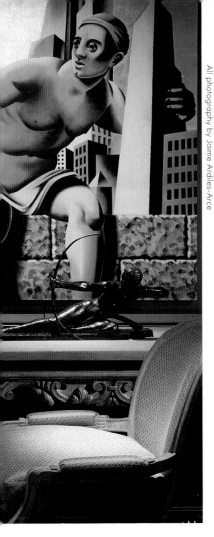

All photography by Jaime Ardiles-Arce

turb my communicating with the art and the feeling of the space?

So, when clients say they must have a dining table and chairs for fourteen, I will usually ask how often they need to seat fourteen people. Why clutter a room for the one or two times each year? Better to do less furniture and buy a beautiful painting which will not only have room to breathe, but also will afford the clients such visual pleasure. I subscribe to the theory of not cluttering up one's home with lots of pieces of furniture, when truly a few pieces will do. I always hope that clients will see the wisdom of having no more than one's lifestyle truly requires.

What's surprising is that I am at the same time a passionate collector. I travel and shop and see much that I would ache to own and enjoy forever. In the past, I have solved this by putting most things away behind closed doors and rotating them from time to time. The downside, however, is that, because I buy only what I truly love, it's heartbreaking to not be able to look at the wonderful objects or art work I have purchased. So, to a great extent, today I must resist buying for my own personal use. Hopefully, we will someday add to our collection of homes and I can then remove my beautiful treasures from hidden confinement.

I am also terribly visual; I have a great need for everything to be beautiful. Even my choice of dogs—adorable wire haired fox terriers—delight my visual senses. I realize that this quest

for visual perfection makes me demanding of the people I work with. But fortunately I am blessed to be surrounded by wonderfully supportive and caring craftsmen, associates, and employees who appreciate and understand that I ask no more of them than of myself. I am equally demanding in terms of quality. I do not compromise. If I would have to compromise quality in order to produce something saleable, then I would simply refrain from producing the item.

In life, you need to come to a point when you know who you are and what it is that you do best, and go with it. I'm quite certain that the very fact that I am so focused and that I demand so much of myself enables me to bring what I hope is good and worthwhile design to so many other people.

bottom right

Another area in my New York showroom surrounds my J. Robert Scott collection of furniture with a Daum chandelier (c. 1928), a Schneider vase (c. 1928), a signed Art Deco bronze, and sterling candlesticks.

Opposite Gottleib's work, nothing conflicts although the pieces are equally significant— Richard Serra's *Untitled* painting (1976), a fourteenth-century Thai vessel, and a wooden female figure from Mali.

bottom left

Our second home in Santa Fe has a slightly different point of view... less pristine, more casual. My husband Bernard Lewis, collects American Indian artifacts which I combine with the emerging artists in my contemporary collection. Among them here are, on the left, David Storey's *Untitled* (1985) and, on the right, Nancy Haynes' *Untitled* (1984).

top left

In the entry, I wanted absolutely no furniture, but I did place a piece I found in Paris, an Egyptian relief in limestone representing amulets of Ptolémée II Philadelphe (285–246 B.C.). On the overdoor is a sculpture by Gregory Mahoney, *Ray #20 Vertical Rain*, (1984–1985). Looking through to the dining room, part of Robert Motherwell's *California Window* (1975) is visible. Lighting for these pieces was a must, and I feel no room in fact talks to you properly without proper illumination.

bottom right

I purchased Adolph Gottleib's *Pink Smash* (1959) five years before I had this house with its ceilings high enough to accommodate such a large painting, and it inspired the way I did the entire interior. It is so powerful that I then needed only linen walls, black leather sofas, wooden floors…nothing else.

Donald Hensman
at home

All photography by © Julius Shulman, Hon. AIA

Modern architecture customarily pays lip service to the concept of total environmental integration—the interdependence of inside and outside. However, all too frequently this concept does not come to fruition, and the glass wall forms a barrier between the highly detailed interior architectural space and the garden-to-be-developed at some future date. In contradiction, this house overlooking Los Angeles and built by me in 1976, represents an attempt by Buff & Hensman FAIA (now Buff, Smith & Hensman) to achieve true spatial integration. The swimming pool, long, narrow and of a constant depth, reflects the linear quality of the house, while the structural module, repeated in the quarry tile terrace patterns and the bridge spanning the pool, serves to unite the south roof terrace and the main body of the house. The sculpture at the southern extreme of the roof deck and the northern edge of the shade terrace terminate the site development and form the major axial visual foci. The site then is developed in total with a continuity of materials, surfaces and forms that strive to establish oneness—a complete unity of design and purpose. The materials vocabulary of the house is extremely restricted—redwood walls, quarry tile flooring, teak cabinetry and natural wool carpeting combine to form a serene, yet simultaneously dramatic environment.

right

I feel very strongly that a building's approach should give you the feeling that something interesting lies ahead.

bottom

The total site...the land...must be considered.

top

Simplicity...simplicity...
simplicity.

bottom

Continuity of landscape,
architecture and interior
is all important.

left

A home should be a series of experiences. To the architect and interior designer, it should demonstrate what can be achieved through massing and creating vignettes.

bottom

Every square inch, especially in one's home, should be...deserves to be...thoughtfully and totally designed.

Antti Nurmesniemi

at work & at home

I have always lived near the place where I have worked. Once my wife, the fashion designer Vuokko, and I built this house, it also meant that I could always "be at home." I do a lot of work late in the evening and into the night, so the border between my working and leisure time and space tends to disappear. Yet, I have learned to appreciate the "studio at home" as a positive solution, because the studio space is quite separate from my home space.

I have always been interested in designing spaces, even though I am an interior and product designer by training and not an architect. In my studio we do varied work from all fields of design...interior design, product design, graphic design....Right now one of our projects, among others, is to design bridges and create aesthetic environments.

As a studio, we are very small scale. I have two assistants and a secretary. Vuokko has her own working space at home and occasionally she participates in some specific project at the studio.

So in our case you can really speak of a studio-home and design family!

Our house is situated on the seashore of Kulosaari island, six kilometers east of Helsinki. The ground level is three hundred and fifty square meters and the second level is one hundred and fifty square meters. The foundation is concrete, with strong water isolation.

We designed it in 1974 and built it in 1975. Our aim was to merge a design studio and living quarters in such a way as to keep them separate, yet make sure that, together, they form a harmonious whole.

Our intention was also to build a practical space for various purposes, allowing a free view out over the sea, with an exterior that would be as simple and straightforward as possible. Taking into consideration the building's site, we avoided too much height. This was not a restriction imposed by building regulations, but our own aesthetic assessment.

A final, important aim was to conserve the property's existing trees, and to plant more once the building was completed.

The solution we developed was a multi-level space that forms a whole entity, where solid walls have been used only to separate washing and upkeeping quarters. The building consists of three interconnecting levels and has no real stories.

I view the industrial arts and design in Europe through Finnish eyes. Where I am standing is way up at the top of

Europe, an attic bedroom, you could say. I come from a northern country. A country which is said to lie between East and West. A land whose seasonal extremes influence our way of life. I have my back to the icy rollers of the Arctic Ocean. Before me, Europe opens up like a huge garden, with the blue Mediterranean glittering in the distance.

For us people of the north, the Arctic Ocean means a coldness and harshness that we ourselves experience. It is a sea that means we need a practical approach. The Mediterranean, on the other hand, is an area of spontaneity and decoration.

Our material world and the form language we use have emerged from a basis of practicality. Our original artifacts were simple and practical, and in their own unassuming way they had a pure beauty. The pattern made on wood was carved with a *puukko* knife; the weave produced in fabric followed the dictates of a simple loom. Our aim was practicality and the beauty inherent in it.

As international links increased, there was an enrichment. The Mediterranean drew closer to the Arctic Ocean. In many respects we have found that our present material environment has been formed out of the meeting and integration of local folk tradition and outside trends.

Today, we designers form part of a multifarious international chain of events. The unavoidable universal problems of energy, raw materials and employment affect the conditions under which planning takes place. As we get

more international, the boundaries between different sectors of culture are in danger of becoming blurred. National values will come in for serious study. The vast responsibility it carries and the importance of human values will underline the significance of creative work at all levels.

The language of design is the language of things and environments. It is a very rich international language with its own dialects. It speaks to us of the level of our culture, the orientation of our technology and of the kind of decisions we have made in developing and cherishing our culture. In their own different ways, the language of design is spoken by coffee cups, cars and houses, advertising posters and street signs, furniture and interiors. The language of design is the non-verbal language of the practical and visual. Its roots delve deeply into local conditions, but its message is universal.

The things we design are an integral part of our everyday life, and of high days and holidays, too. In things, we give material form to functional need. They variously show an emphasis on aesthetic values or functional beauty. It is the task of us designers to integrate human values into what are sometimes highly technical products.

I have often heard it said that the current process of internationalization is refining, simplifying and standardizing industrially produced goods and the things we use. Such talk has always scared me. It is true that mass production cannot follow the complex and subtle tradition of individual handicraft. However, this does not have to mean

All photography by Ilmari Kostiainen/Klikki

top

Dining space.

bottom

Winter elevation.

merciless standardization. What is more, the industrial mechanism is already so highly developed that it can be used much more freely than it is now. Mastering the technology does not have to mean doing things in a particular way. On the other hand, not understanding the technology makes us its slaves.

It seems to me that in the near future the built environment will increasingly be made up of parts and components that are industrially produced. Thus, the role played by industrially produced small goods will also grow. Our level of industrial development has reached a point at which the public is ready to accept the industrial product as a self-evident feature of our age. We are not afraid of duplication. We accept products that are serially produced—for one reason, because the production method makes them cheap.

Even so, we expect things to have "humanized" qualities. Perhaps that is why handmade things are in such demand. The fact that the value and appreciation of handicrafts is increasing all the time does not mean that a revolution is going on, but it is a clear indication that people are dissatisfied with excessive industrialization. But the handmade is an alternative, not an inevitability. I believe that the advance of handicrafts will play its part in raising the quality of industrially-produced goods. Industry will have to examine its own attitude to the human quality of what it produces.

opposite

Living room.

top

Living room.

center

With my assistant Jorma Valkama.

bottom

Stair to gallery.

Agustin Hernandez N.

at work & at home

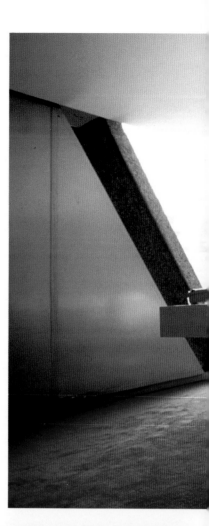

A workshop should not only be a refuge against the external environment, or a place where a man can work. Its spaces should induce him to act through optic perception. Every architectural project should take into account, as an important factor, the spectator's emotional manifestation and the impressions transmitted through spaces and form.

Geometry, as an exact science of space relation and the technical development of various forms, offers an enormous field for architectural possibilities. By facing these various forms, we will achieve a harmony in statics, aesthetics and economy expressing the architect's conception.

A prismatic triangular module was used in this project, my studio in Mexico City where I live and work. Some of the technical problems in the development of creativity may be solved through the understanding of natural structures, which have become of great importance in architectural projects. Thus, on a 45-degree sloped, wooded lot we chose an organic solution to blend with the landscape. The trunk of the tree-shaped building has an anchoring foundation, similar to tree roots, with great anti-seismic qualities.

Two strained polyhedric modules and two in compression form the top foliage. A reinforced concrete structure with marble aggregates was used to achieve similar interiors and exteriors.

We sought a structural sobriety to emphasize each one of its elements and to achieve the optimum in construction with the most adequate space distribution within a functional interdependence.

bottom right

Our kinetic overview has replaced our perception abilities with other abilities which require more dynamic forms.

top

Having my studio close to where I live and sleep enables me to have my drawing tools at hand whenever an idea emerges, so I can try to capture it at its most profound level.

bottom

My small library is full of different visual angles. A crystal glass table is illuminated by a dome which looks to the sky and through which I can see the stairway that leads to my workshop.

John F. Saladino

at home

Photography by Andrew Kohler

P rofessionally, interior design, when it is practiced as fine art and at its highest level, will allow us moments of transcendence. We can emotionally and spiritually be renewed through the design of our environments, but only when those environments address needs beyond shelter. Rooms are not only to keep the rain off our heads, or to cool us, or to warm us. They should nurture us emotionally.

When we walk into a room we should be exhilarated, as though we are experiencing something for the first time. The interior is not a six-sided box with a floor, a ceiling and four walls that we then stuff with furnishings. First of all, the proportions of a room should be in perfect harmony. Like musicians who have perfect pitch, interior designers should have at their disposal the talent and training that enables them to create perfect harmony.

A sense of repose is what I personally seek. I like rooms that are serene. *How do you do that?* Well, I always tell clients it is more important what you leave out than what you put in. As a designer my dialogue is with the "space in between."

I am concerned with the interior as a "walk-in" still life and the silhouette of a chair in juxtaposition with the mantle or the wall.

In a room, light is the prime mover. No space is worth human occupation without natural light. Think about all the windowless kitchens and bathrooms in which people spend years of their lives trapped. We should not live in filing cabinets.

Interiors should be built to last. All the veneers that are so available in all the contract showrooms are not the materials to which we return. As Americans, we journey to Europe often to admire buildings and rooms that were made to endure. I cannot imagine crossing the Atlantic to admire a fake paneled room with quarter-inch thick marble floors.

If the interior can be fine art, then we interior designers have in our control the ability to enhance life and to elevate us from the caves from which we came.

The design philosophy in my New York apartment was to create a contrast between the corroded taupe "scratch coat" plaster walls of the drawing room and the refined smooth lacquered mauve walls of the adjacent bedroom. A comparison would be a seashell which is barnacled on the outside and smooth like lingerie on the inside. I wanted the drawing room, with its vast three-story high dimensions, to evoke permanence in a city that exists on constant change.

All photography except where noted by Lizzie Himmel

Photography by William Waldron

Victoria Hagan
at work & at home

Photography by © Andrew Garn

YOU have to respect your space and approach it in design terms with a certain integrity. From that attitude the interior evolves.

I think what is similar between my office and my home is my attitude toward simplicity and space. In my home, it's important that it be a serene retreat. One reason I chose my particular apartment in New York is the softness of its southern light.

I also love to collect. I've created a neutral backdrop so I can continue collecting from all periods and countries. Yet, there is a relationship among the different forms, and that makes the combination a bit unexpected.

I'm always searching for the unusual, and when I'm designing for myself I can be a bit more experimental than when designing for clients. However, in all my design, including work for clients, I like everything to be fresh...not to have been done before. And I think this can be achieved using antiques.

One reason I like this approach is that it leaves the door open for endless variations. I change my home continually, depending on my direction at any particular moment.

As does my home, the offices of Feldman-Hagan Interiors have high ceilings and plenty of windows. Only here, they allow a northern exposure, which I consider better for working.

Again, there's a sense of spaciousness...the walls are white and in a state of constant evolution because of the unusual pieces I am always purchasing for clients.

I think it's as important for the office to have a sense of serenity as it is for the home. Even if it's not always true, I try to create the illusion of calm. The happy thing is that the illusion exudes a calming feeling; the illusion becomes reality.

top left

In my apartment where storage space is tight, I find room for additional books here on top of my Michael Graves stool.

top right

The reflection from the mirror, custom designed to look old, makes the space brighter.

center left

In my office as well as my home, I have a collection of accessories...such as this silverleaf dish...and flowers. I go to the Flower District early in the morning about once each week and come back with enough for three or four bouquets, which I arrange myself.

center right

Again, in my office, simplicity. At the entryway, a Larry Fink photograph is juxtaposed with only a French Empire walnut table, a Venetian chair and an iron bench.

bottom right

I was attracted to this office space because of the high ceilings and northern light.

Photography by © Andrew Garn

Photography by © Andrew Garn

top right

My kitchen is tiny, but it's open and light. The small restaurant range makes the room feel larger. It's an illusion, because one would think you would need a spacious kitchen to do this.

bottom left

I debated over whether or not to keep the faux mantlepiece in my apartment. Conceptually, I don't like the idea of its being fake, but then I decided I needed it to serve as a focal point. I enjoy changing my arrangements over and within it. At the moment, I have some of the favorite pieces I've collected—a German silverplate vase and a piece of pottery from the 1920s. I think of the mixture as a collage; there's always a relationship between one piece and another.

bottom right & top left

What I like best about the possessions in my apartment is that they become very graphic. I especially like my collection of miniature furniture. They all have their own personality and are displayed in a way that emphasizes the juxtaposition of scale. I also like the contrast of the rare with the humble; there is no set of rules that one must follow. You simply must trust your own eye.

Jill I. Cole
at work & at home

Originally I wanted to build, but I couldn't find a piece of property in the location in Los Angeles I wanted. I moved here from a house designed by architect Jerry Lomax, the type of space I'm drawn to—very white and symmetrical—a good background. I put that house up for sale during the last frenzied real estate market and it sold quickly. I bought this place in Beverly Hills in haste, needing to move fast, and now I've been here for twelve years, always threatening to move again.

Just "whitening" the space was critical to me. Light is so important, I get very depressed in places without a lot of it. I am strongly affected by environment. Every time I start a new house I say "O.K., this time I'm going to put color into it." But in the end I've never been able to do it.

A neutral background allows the art, not the interior, to become the focus, and having been a fine arts major, I am attracted to art and the process of making it. As long as I can remember I have bought, sold and collected art. Over the years my tastes have changed, beginning with more "painterly" work and evolving through pop and abstract expressionism. Currently, I have become increasingly interested in three-dimensional work and contemporary photography.

In addition, I find white spaces best for entertaining, allowing me to set the mood with accessories, food or lighting unhindered by assertive design elements or color schemes. In my house, even a flower arrangement can effectively set the desired scene, affording me the visual variety I desire.

In the office of Cole Martinez Curtis and Associates in Marina del Rey, California, I'm again surrounded by expanses of white and open spaces. The office is a renovated supermarket on the Grand Canal. Ten years ago, our firm agreed to occupy the old Safeway building because it presented possibilities unheard of in conventional office space. For one thing, the building had no center core. Because the twenty-five-thousand-square foot ground floor forms an almost perfect square, interrupted only by a minimal number of columns, the principals could occupy the center, along with conference areas. Each principal has a secretary sitting immediately outside the office and the various departments radiate from there in open work stations.

With no private offices on the windows, a maximum amount of daylight is shared by all. Clerestories and a skylight supplement the available natural light. The skylight is located above an inner courtyard/conference area in the middle of the principals' offices, which serves as an area for internal meetings as well as client conferences. After business hours, the "courtyard" is a place for administrative meetings and relaxation.

My own office reflects my philosophy of simplicity and classicism. There are clean lines wherever you look from the desk to the classic Joseph Hoffman pull-up chairs. But look closely—as I finally used color on the padded silk walls—yet it's so subtle that even I scarcely notice it.

All photography by Toshi Yoshimi

top

In my personal office space, I like literally nothing to interfere with the creative process.

right

White, light, open spaces—Cole Martinez Curtis renovated an old supermarket, taking advantage of possibilities unheard of in conventional office space.

left

In my living room, the art is the focus: Hannah Wilke's rubber sculpture above the fireplace; Claes Oldenburg's *Baked Potato* and *Rye Crisp* on the tables; Mark Lere's bronze sculpture. The furniture I view as art too: from the round cocktail table by Eileen Gray to the antique African tribal stool.

bottom

For entertaining, I change the mood through accessories and flowers. Ready for guests here are: Mitsukoshi service plates, antique silver, Waterford crystal, Pratesi linens, and Antique Knights in Armor centerpiece from James Robinson. The silver teapot on the sideboard is a piece from Memphis Milano.

Anna Castelli
Ferrieri

at home

top left

My portrait is an oil painting by Roberto Sambonet.

bottom

As we go nearer we see, at middle height in the first bookcase, a shelf with some precious vases and objects. The cans on the small table are full of shells and marble eggs I found around the world.

opposite

This is a view, taken from a passage, of the wall of my sleeping room, where I have my small collection of minor but important Italian painters like DePisis, Migneco, Baj, Campigli and DeChirico, who designed a costume for my father who was a theater director and critic.

My life is long and rich in works that go across all aspects of design, from city-planning to architecture and industrial design. I don't think the approach to design changes in tackling these different dimensions. What may change is that, as the focus gets nearer the individual use, the project starts losing its direct connection to the physical context. Production multiplies and is destined to everybody, simply to man, which may lead to the optimistic conclusion that men are more equal than you may believe. Of course, I do not believe that all men are equal, but I'm satisfied when I satisfy the desires or I meet the needs of the many people who have the same expectations I have and when I get a reply to my message.

Industrial design is the work to which I devoted most of my time during the last few years and that I have also been teaching at Milan University, at the Domus Academy in Milan and at the RMIT in Melbourne. There is a definite reason for this choice: in my opinion the project is the most intense way to communicate with people, to send a message which has to get an answer, but, industrial design in particular represents the quickest and most reliable way to get this answer from a great number of persons living in all sides of the world.

I must say I work very seldom on interior design; I do it for office buildings whose architecture I have also designed and in the case of very close friends or relatives, for whom I am just dealing with the general interior architectural layout. In fact, I think that a private home cannot be conceived all at the same time, but that it should be born little by little, following the traditions of the owner, his changing wishes and needs, his memories and his dreams, thus allowing everybody to express his own character and atmosphere. None of us has been born under a cabbage; maybe a grandfather of ours has left a simple object that he loved and this is a reason for us to love it too and not to throw it away.

I think everybody is recognizable through his house. In my case, I designed the building myself, searching for a site in front of an ancient park, which is something rare in my town of Milan. I have a small apartment that tells a lot about me and my life.

First, it is full of books: books are everywhere. One of the bookcases which is near to the windows is meant to be dedicated to glass objects: there the light goes through the glass and enhances colors and transparencies. This is not a collection, but there are pieces that I found here and there and that I brought home because I loved them: the most important piece is the vase *Altair* by Ettore Sottsass.

Only some pieces of furniture are designed by me: the fiberglass dining table, a revolving bookcase and the small tables near the sofas (we call them stoobles because they are stools and tables at the same time). There are also some planters and a revolving TV stand, which allow me to transform a large part of my living room into a garden that is visually connected with the park outside.

I have some family antiques, some Thonet chairs and some paintings, but only a few, because the walls are all covered with books.

The remaining furniture is designed by contemporary designers. What I like most is that my home doesn't reveal itself as an architect's home, but rather as a home of a person who has certain cultural interests that keep the house alive.

My office is quite the same except that the changing items are drawings and models and the signals of ongoing work, which, as I already said, is quite multi-faceted.

My office, too, is full of books.

opposite

In the entry room, two photographs of my grandfathers are on the folding door; a ceramic cat by Agenore Fabbri (one of the best known Italian sculptors and a friend of mine) sits on the small revolving bookcase; and on the table at the right are two old Chinese vases

top

The two wicker armchairs; on the wall a famous painting by Asger Yorn.

center top

This is a general view of the living room. From left to right: a bookcase, a second stand with glass objects, a fireplace, a TV set, two wicker armchairs; foreground, two sofas covered with linen velvet. The pig near the chimney is a design of mine for Matteo Grassi, so is the TV stand and the stools for Kartell.

center bottom

Bookcases on the opposite wall; a shelf for magazines and new books, an antique adjustable quartet music stand with four candles and reading shelves.

bottom

Details of the glass objects in the second bookcase and a view of the column bordering the fireplace that varies in depth so as to be able to contain the chimney, books of different size, some small cabinets, and shelves for some objects. On this side there are books and some old prints; on the opposite one there are small family portraits in golden frames. The lamp is by Ettore Sottsass.

Francois Catroux

at home

In my terrace garden on the site of the former Hotel de Condé, where my dream of a tour de force for my apartment's interior began.

In the sitting room, my interest in architecture is reflected in cornice and wall panels molded in staff to imitate the building's exterior. The carpet which runs throughout my apartment was inspired by the marble foyer of the Théâtre de l'Odéon nearby.

My apartment is among the fine classical residences that were built in the eighteenth century on the site of the former Hotel de Condé and near the Théâtre de l'Odéon in Paris. Its garden on one side and courtyard on the other are as perfect as stage sets and inspired me to create an interior that would echo my home's historic circumstances in an equally theatrical manner. My image was not grandeur itself so much as the dream of grandeur.

The material central to my theme was the use of staff, a mixture of plaster of Paris and cement. A temporary building material, it provided another way of expressing how we all are forever surrounding ourselves with our dreams.

Since my taste usually runs toward extreme Modernism, it was natural for my interpretation of the past to take on an unusual perspective, almost supernatural. I never lost sight of the concept that one would be viewing the past from today. I wanted to condense centuries and set them in relief, one against the other.

For those architectural elements I built of staff, I exaggerated their scale and stripped them of the ornamentation that would have been theirs historically. Broken cornices in the sitting room, embossed walls there and in the hall and bathroom, even a concrete staircase in the bedroom recall the city's exterior elements rather than a residential interior.

I like the drama of a few strong images, too, a drama heightened by their relationship with each other—such as the sitting room's huge bronze bird by Czaki and the mighty torso of Atlas. Yet, I never like the end result to seem "noisy." I prefer much more for a room to be underdone rather than filled to the brim. I like the feeling of abstraction, like a not-quite-completed canvas. Thus, my use of color is restrained or non-existent, and my accessorization is edited until much that remains can be seen in silhouette rather than in busy clusters.

For, in fact, the furnishings that do remain are quite solid design, indeed excellent. From Georges Jacob's bookcases and table in the dining room, to Boulard's chairs in the sitting room, to the pieces by Mies van der Rohe and Mauser, each is outstanding in design, material and fabrication and has been chosen with great care and much admiration. And, despite my garden and courtyard being so perfect that they don't seem real, I adore drinking in the reality of their beauty. In the end, you might say I like the reality within the unreality.

In the television room, walls lined with brown felt and covered with nineteenth century architectural plans of Egyptian temples are flanked by a pair of columns made of molded staff. A large Sevres vase with mythological pattern also carries forth the theme of antiquity.

right

In the library/dining room, a pair of eighteenth-century coromandel lacquer screens and a pair of bookcases by Georges Jacob form a symmetrical arrangement around the fireplace. Draped canvas curtains lead to the rooms beyond.

top

Adding excitement to the
entry hall's white painted
walls are two pieces from
Indonesia, a throne chair
and an urn in the shape
of a bull.

Photography by Terris Guell

Orlando Diaz-Azcuy

at work

The spaces where I live and work have to be very peaceful and act as a background for self-generated energy—the complete opposite of the energetic spaces so many people like. I like a space to work and serve as background for people and what they do. That does not necessarily mean it has to be a white canvas. But, the colors, furnishings and details, no matter how rich or ornate, should not be more important than the people.

In my own office, made up of three buildings joined together on San Francisco's Maiden Lane, I have worked with the spatial quality of the volumes and furnishings so that it would be neither all hard-edged nor, in terms of furnishings, overwhelming. I wanted lots of space around me, but I also wanted it to feel like home to me and to the people with whom I work and our clients. In fact, my home is really very much the same but in a different vocabulary. It is located in a 1913 building in which the clean appearance of the spaces, even though there are strong architectural details, allows them to serve as a background.

My interest in the past is normally reflected in antiques. Antiques often provide elements of interest in all my work, as they certainly do in my office and home, only my home is absolutely full of them.

Yet, primarily that which defines good architecture and design is function. I dislike very much to do something only because it looks good. If a space doesn't work, I feel I have accomplished nothing. So, it is only after I have taken care of the function that I free myself to consider other venues of expression and enhancement.

Function depends very much on clear organization. It is important to me that the sequence of spaces, rooms and activities be clearly organized so that people can live or work in them with a minimal amount of wasted energy and in a logical manner.

Regarding light—no matter what you have, if you do not see it properly, you do not have it. One of my theories is that color in spaces should relate more to the quality of light than to the capricious desire of having certain colors. This also applies to the use and control of natural lighting. For example, in my own office, the presentation room has a large window at one end which would have looked like a light at the end of a tunnel were it not

for the two mirrors that reflect and expand its illumination.

In addition to function, vitally important to me is the consideration of spatial volume. The size of a space beyond what is necessary for function is not as important to me as its volume. In fact, today in the remodeling of older houses, there is much enlarging going on without any consciousness of what is being destroyed or what awkward volumes are being created. The uplifting quality of a space with a high ceiling cannot be replaced by that of a larger room with a low ceiling.

One of the reasons that I selected this building for our office was the variety of spaces and volumes throughout. In other words, there is not one constant ceiling height. In a room in which the proportions are not right, one must compensate. In the case of my overly long presentation room, I added five vertical elements and angled the ceiling at one end to modulate and give interest to the space.

I like to think in terms of interior architecture. I try to design the entire space from the floor, to what's above me, to what's beside me. I am constantly appreciating the relationship of the three dimensional. It is very typical that designers are too concerned with the amount of furniture they want in a space rather than its relationship to the space.

However, the architecture of a building must be respected when one is creating rooms. We should be very careful how rooms relate to a building in its totality. It is not always possible to place a period room within a structure built today. Too often, people think they can solve the problem by enriching with architectural detail, but the result is a mummy-like room that doesn't come alive. In older buildings, when all those columns and pediments were designed, the bones of the entire building went with them. Architectural ornamentation should only be added when the room's bones are correct for it. Otherwise, the room should be left as simple as possible. One can still bring in art and artifacts for the desired gesture to the past.

Frank Lloyd Wright had the rare opportunity of designing not only buildings but all the furnishings and details within. Right now, I am privileged to be doing that, in one case designing even the electrical plugs. But, such a chance usually comes once in a lifetime. One has to accept the fact that one must work within a given space or with some other pre-existing condition and respect it rather than thwart it and wind up with some ungainly juxtaposition.

Good design can truly make a difference in people's well-being. In my experience, I find I react very emotionally to what I see, and very much in the same manner as other physical experiences. While mediocre design can feel oppressive, to observe, work and live in wonderful environments uplifts my entire life.

top right

Passage between the reception area and my office and presentation room. Both sides and ceiling are mirrored.

opposite

Entry stairs lead from the street to the reception room and continue to the upstairs office. Stairs on the right lead toward my private office and presentation room. The panel is eighteenth-century French in the style of Watteau; the green pagoda bee-keep is from a chateau in France; the rug is Samarkand.

opposite

View of the reception room with conference room in the background showing the Corvo chair I designed for Steelcase. In the foreground are two Chalice chairs in gold from the collection I designed for Hickory Business Furniture. They were presented to the public at the Armory opening in New York. Also shown are a Samarkand rug, a Regency wrought iron and stone table and two Cav. Piranesi F. etchings, circa 1775.

top

In my office and presentation room, five vertical elements and angled ceiling compensate for the proportions of the overly long room. The nineteenth-century Chinese bed export for the French market is combined with an all-leather screen, a French Neo-classic marble architectural piece, Rainbow chairs I designed, and a Gae Aulenti table from Knoll International. The rug is Samarkand.

the Earth Spirits

All photography by John Vaughan

Joszi Meskan
at work & at home

top right

At the entry to my office, there is a ladder that goes nowhere. That is the mystery as well as the good news, because one has already climbed twenty steps in this south of Market warehouse. Inside the Chinese bowl are curious, fossilized, bark-covered balls that came from the Philippines.

bottom

Illuminated by the special light coming through the industrial windows are reproduction Biedermeier chairs covered with printed cowhide atop an all black carpet.

I don't think of my home in terms of design, though naturally harmony and balance do exist, or I wouldn't be happy here! It's more a matter of personal expression than a conscious effort to convey some kind of image to other people. Everything here means something to me. Every object has a story connected with it, or gives me a good, positive, spiritual feeling.

My piano teacher says you can play for two reasons...for other people, to entertain and please them, or because you have a deep need to express yourself through music. Precision and timing and technique are important in either case, but when you are playing for yourself, you try and try again to find out what the composer wanted to say, and you derive a deep inner pleasure from the spiritual communication.

That's what my Pacific Heights home in San Francisco means to me. It's an expression...it feels very harmonious...and when I look at something, it's very interesting when viewed objectively, and it nurtures my sense of communication with whoever created it.

Some objects are ancient and valuable, hallowed by time. Others are simply old and loved, worn smooth by handling. Some are exotic, some humble in origin. A few were created yesterday. But, each object has been a part of someone's life, and is now a part of mine.

My business life, at Joszi Meskan Associates, is conducted in a very different environment, albeit a peaceful one. So much business, so much emotion, the needs of so many high-powered people, demand that the background should provide a stage for all the performers—clients and designers alike.

I would say that in both my office and my home, different though they are, there's a sense of spirit as well as of technique, and I know this is true of all my best work. I now finally recognize that at the root of my work there is a

true sensuality. That's perhaps an over-used word, but it's the essense of connecting the feeling with technique, making spaces beautiful as well as useful.

To be able to do that well is really a gift, and I have a strong feeling that the talented Clive Kahn, who worked with me until his death in 1984, placed his talent in trust with me. I feel that I have to use it carefully and, when through, somehow pass it on. Before Clive died, I felt as if I had to follow the rules...to match and balance, and not have anything out of place. But in the past eight years, I've found that a little strangeness in the proportions, a slight bending of the accepted rules, a relaxation of the tension is accepted and understood, not intellectually but sensually. People do respond without one having to define exactly what one is doing. This happens as you become more confident that you can please your own eye, and that other people will respond because we all have our share of the same feelings. I love that feeling of being able to connect with someone through my work on an emotional and spiritual level instead of just via an intellectual analysis of space.

I decided to leave the structural heart of this light industrial building exposed, and, even though there is about two thousand five hundred square feet of space, there are no walls separating any of the "rooms." Among the visual dividers are cabinets housing an extensive library of several thousand books, which also serve as a backdrop for the receptionist station. The pelicans I rescued from a job site in Burma. The reproduction Biedermeier chairs are from Spain.

top left

Thatcher was my fiftieth year present. He's the child I never had. Johnny, my carpenter of eighteen years, built him this house with skylights and windows that open. It's a splendid piece of real estate — but Thatcher never uses it!

top right

The screen above my headboard shows one monkey holding hands with another stretching to catch the crab on the ground. That's what I see when I wake up in the morning. I love the linen damask cover on the bed…the Chippendale tea table that I found in England. It holds whatever books I am reading, and personal photographs. Forward of that are Japanese-influenced chairs…over the arm of one is a handwoven Afghan blanket in a wonderful lettuce green color. Then there's my little luggage stand and the Indonesian woven-leather-and-rattan duffle bag I always have handy for quick packing. Underneath I store my exercise weights.

bottom

I like this Bruce Lauritzen acrylic painting because it's so naive, as are so many of the objects I've acquired…the carved leopard table in the foreground has an ancient Ethiopian Bible with the original wooden cover sitting on it. The Bible is entirely hand written in tiny, neat characters. All the small objects here, like the warthog and the elephant, were created by artists from various regions in Africa. A number of galleries are now commissioning African artists to continue this tradition of hand carving in ebony, a fantastically hard wood. The Africans who live with the wildlife really understand the animals' bodies. To the left of the fireplace is a spear presented to me by a Masai warrior.

Photography by Eitan Feinholz

Gerard Pascal and Carlos Pascal
at work & at home

We were born in Montevideo, Uruguay, and we lived there all of our adolescence which is a very important formative period. Montevideo is a small city by the sea, and it has a strong European influence, especially Spanish and Italian. Basically, it is an old-looking city, its last prosperous period being the years following World War II when it was called "The Switzerland of America." After that, recession, social confrontation and economic instability slowed development and many of the younger people emigrated to other lands looking for better opportunities.

Living there was a joyful experience and the aged city by the sea engraved a strong image of brick houses with a worn look, the *rambla* (promenade) and the long walks by the beach. We remember the *confiterias* (coffee and pastries shops) very similar to the ones in Europe with their smell of fresh coffee, the downtown area with its colonial buildings, and the Montevideo harbor with its fortress. There we could see the big ships coming and leaving.

Enhancing all these aspects of life there was the noticeable difference in the changing seasons—the cold and grey winter, the happily beautiful spring with the blooming trees and the butterflies, summer with its heat and constant trips to the beach, autumn with the red of the falling leaves and the *Vendimia* or feast of the harvesting of the grapes and making of new wine. All of these experiences, when left, were kept inside ourselves with the innocence of youth. So for us it will never change.

We left Uruguay in 1972 and moved north.

Mexico was a new learning experience in every way: the place, the people, the food, the way of living. Immediately we began studying at the university, but as we had just arrived at this country, it was like a vacation. This makes perception of things more open…nothing seems routine…every day we were doing something new.

We traveled extensively throughout the country to the old towns and haciendas, convents, ruins. Every place seemed so authentic…its vernacular architecture reflecting the use of indigenous materials found on site, its daily life incorporating traditions from pre-Hispanic times. If something works, then it is kept forever in this simple but rich culture…this is the lesson that Mexico, with its high moral values and

family loving society, teaches us every minute of every day. People here are very friendly, so they have made it easy for us to adapt to this new environment.

Carlos is thirty-five years old. He is married to Gaby, who is Mexican, and they have two little boys, Daniel who is three years old, and Mark who is one-and-a-half.

I am Gerard. I am thirty-seven years old. I am married to Sara who also is Mexican and we have two children also, Ian who is three and Philippe who is one-and-a-half. Both of our wives are graphic designers.

Carlos and I work twelve hours daily except on weekends when Carlos leaves for his house in Yautepec, an hour's drive from the city, and its warm weather and spectacular views. There he enjoys his gardening and bike riding.

On weekends, my family and I go to Valle de Bravo, two hours away from Mexico City. Located in the mountains at a beautiful lake where we sail, Valle de Bravo is a small colonial town with stucco houses all painted white and with terra cotta roofs. It is cold at night there, and there are great places to walk with woods, creeks and waterfalls showing nature at its best.

Nature at its best—this has a lot to do with the way Carlos and I design, as I will explain.

We founded Pascal Arquitectos in 1979. Today, we are dedicated to architectural projects and high-end interior design. We don't have a particular style. We like almost every period, recognizing good things in every one of them. This allows us to join into a new design experience with every client we have. We like the classical touch and the use of natural materials, of course. And being young makes us contemporary in the way of feeling design. But, we like the calm and sense of assurance that traditional styles communicate.

Having an architectural background makes us pay special attention to the decoration lent by the basic architecture itself. Antiques and good art will always find a place in our projects, but we are also aware of how light and shadow themselves help create rooms

and form their character.

We believe in the classical order of architecture and we apply it to the contemporary. We want to be fashionable but not trendy. We like our projects to last and we think that linking them to the past provides a sense of comfort and a relaxed look that can be luxurious and inviting at the same time.

To advance our understanding of this constantly developing philosophy, we travel and we study every book we can get our hands on. We subscribe to every architecture and interior design magazine that we know of and we literally devour all this information with great pleasure.

We built two religious buildings which not only gave us much pride but also a spiritual gratification. We saw people praying in rooms we had created from images in our minds…a serious responsibility and a great honor.

We have a staff of fourteen, seven being architects. All are experienced and enthusiastic about what they do, which makes it enjoyable to work together. We have a good team. The design style of our offices is similar to that of our own homes, which I would describe as new colonial or contemporary colonial. We incorporate traditional arched patios, corridors, niches, terraces with wrought iron handrails, stone walls, wood-beamed rooves and extensive use of red brick masonry. This is a little different from what we do for our clients, which is more high end and luxurious. We feel that, with us being so involved with design, the places in which we live should not be statements of modern architecture. Instead, we believe they should be softer, a comfortable and subtle mix of details that we like and which inspire us. Above all, perhaps, we believe they should reflect the nature of the geography and culture in which we live.
—*Gerard Pascal*

top left

In our office, my brother Carlos Pascal, left, and myself.

top right

Facade of Pascal Arquitectos.

top

Main Lobby, Front Desk
of Pascal Arquitectos.

bottom

Conference Room, Pascal
Arquitectos.

Facade of Gerard Pascal
residence, view from the
garden.

top right

Terrace, Gerard Pascal
Residence.

bottom

Living Room, Gerard
Pascal Residence.

opposite

Main Hall, Gerard
Pascal Residence.

top

Main Hall, Carlos Pascal
Residence, Mexico City.

bottom

Facade, Carlos Pascal
Residence, Mexico City.

opposite

Main Entrance, Carlos
Pascal vacation home in
Yautepec.

Photography by Lourdes Legorreta

Ricardo Legorreta

at work & at home

I do not leave my work at the office or my play at home. Instead, I see both as one principled, colorful, deeply-rooted whole.

From the selection of the land to the last design detail, I have created an easy work environment—the main goal being to avoid stress and traffic. The site is near the edge of Mexico City and offers a panoramic view with a steep inclination of approximately forty-five degrees. The simplicity of my design approach allows it to adapt gracefully to the land and exude more the feeling of a studio than an office.

The space has been in a continuous state of remodeling since its initial completion in 1966. The principal elements are the reception area, drawing workshop and meeting room. The work spaces were designed at the lowest part of the site, and access is provided through a succession of stairs, patios

The exterior of the house is painted the same color as the earth. No professional landscaping was done, instead I encourage local, natural vegetation to grow randomly and practically cover our house.

All windows were conceived from the inside, according to the views and light I desired to lend the right ambience to each room. I made no formal study whatsoever regarding the design of the facade. This decision came directly from my personal design beliefs. and walls that make the distance an interesting plastic experience. Throughout, there is color—those vibrantly rich hues that distinguish my projects, including my weekend home.

The architectural themes I selected for Casa Valle de Bravo were integration with the landscape, informality and flexibility. The roof, built in the traditional vernacular architecture of the area, follows the slope of the hill, so as to make half of the home situated below ground. By the creation of three platforms, the main elements of the house unfold naturally from living area, to master bedroom, to the children's rooms. There is no furniture in the children's rooms. This allows us greater flexibility with the space, and provides sleeping accommodations for guests—a constant occurrence in the life of this exuberant household.

Legorreta Arquitectos
Architecture and Landscape Architecture: Legorreta Arquitectos, Ricardo Legorreta, Noe Castro, Carlos Vargas

Structural Design: Bernardo Calderon, Jose Luis Calderon

HOW I DESIGN

Each person has his or her own way of doing things, especially when it is a creative activity. For me, the most important matter in designing is to establish a design philosophy. Each building needs and should have its own appropriate principle that directs the design.

When I receive a commission, my life starts spinning around it. I think it, I see it, and I live it. I spend several weeks without drawing or sketching. During this time I think all day about the project, while dressing, eating, listening to music, and especially while looking at books and visiting places of inspiration that have some relation to the problem. Sometimes, I visit similar projects, but this is principally to study technical and functional matters.

Little by little the philosophy of the building starts to take shape in my mind and suddenly I have the feeling that it is ready. Then I draw. When that moment comes I feel a very special excitement. I feel like taking the pencil and I start drawing lines, squares, circles and shapes...and the piece of paper becomes alive, my imagination flies, the shapes are created, and architecture appears. This is the moment of inspiration!

The intellectual approach to architecture, the one that needs explanation, often does not help shape a good building. The intellectual approach restricts the imagination and destroys the emotions that are so important in creating architecture. The process can be compared with love: intellectual love does not forgive, emotional love has deep roots. Spontaneity in designing leaves a trace of the designer's feelings and releases the observer's own imagination to dream with architecture. Usually, I dream color, walls, intimacy, mystery, and other qualities that matter in particular to me as a person, and as a Mexican.

I develop the sketches that represent the philosophy for the building, and it is only when I have a solution that I like philosophically that I start to study the program in detail with regard to function and other prosaic matters. When I have plans, sections, and elevations that reflect philosophical and functional requirements, I ask my people to make models, and once I like the concepts, the process of development starts, aided by an associate architect and my wonderful model-making team. From then on, a continuous follow-up takes place.

Photography by Lourdes Legorreta

I see every detail, from master plan to light fixtures and doorknobs. That is the scope of architecture.

I love to go to the construction site, too. Before that, the building is just drawings. At the construction site architecture takes place. My reward as an architect is when I go alone to the construction site and experience the spaces, light, color—the architecture that is emerging. (Also, sometimes, more often than I like, I experience my mistakes.) This is when I realize I have the most beautiful profession in the world. It allows me to think spiritually. I believe something a friend said to me: "Give thanks because in your profession you have the great opportunity of participating in the completion of God's creation."

Ricardo Legorreta ● at home

Photography by Arthur Coleman

Steve Chase
at work & at home

Photography by Marc Glassman

What I really like to have most in my own home is no longer completely defined by my primary home, which I built nearby my office in Rancho Mirage, California. I work so hard and so much, that I have, especially in later years, not utilized my home as much as I should. On the other hand, I have a second home at the beach in Del Mar which has proved to be a wonderful retreat for me and where I actually spend more time. And, I didn't even build it.

Everything's different between my beach house and my home in Rancho Mirage. The Rancho Mirage home has architectural beauty. Really, it's an elegant piece of thought and design, as appropriate in scale and color as a piece of art. The house at the beach is a condominium, built like so many others. But...it's cozy...it's filled with my treasures, some of which go together and some which do not. It's filled with my childhood and my past, my collections and my stuff. Yet, if a client lived

like this, I would ask him if he had a truck to get rid of it all!

My Rancho Mirage home is significant because it shows clients what I can do. Its quality is impressive and its furnishings...well, it's like a beautiful store. My home in Del Mar I show to very few people and only to those who would understand. The average businessman would run out the door pleading mercy.

You see, I'm not as perfect a person as my Rancho Mirage house would make me appear. Not that I didn't love doing it...creating it...really there are a lot of ideas in that house. But I moved into it from a rambling Spanish house which was one of my favorite houses ever. When I moved into the Rancho Mirage house, that was one of my favorite houses ever, too. But you change. The rambling Spanish house was all charm, no sense. The Rancho Mirage house is all sense and no charm, at least not as much. The next house I do for myself will be a combination of the two.

I suppose one of the main reasons I feel like this is that I live alone and the Rancho Mirage house is big—eleven thousand square feet. And, it's filled with modern abstract paintings. I've discovered in my later years that I really like other things, too, all sorts of things, and I like to have them around me. In Del Mar, I have my collection of model ships and passenger ship memorabilia.... In fact I have to admit that I have come to enjoy the comfortable realism of my thirty-inch-square Franz Bischoff landscape painting, which I keep in my Del Mar house, more than my seventeen-foot-long Helen Frankenthaler or Sam Francis, which I keep in my Rancho Mirage house. I like to have these other things around me now...and I don't want to sleep anymore in a twenty-foot by thirty-foot room with a fifteen-foot-high ceiling.

I would actually like to be in a house one-third the size of my Rancho Mirage house. I'm not interested anymore in making a statement. I needed

right

View into my own office.

Photography by Arthur Coleman

top

Lobby

bottom

A detail of Steve Chase Associates' accessory shop.

the big house to show the world I was here to stay...but that was twelve years ago.

Besides, I always trust I'm going to do something new, not some compendium of everything I've done before but something really new. And what I do in the future won't be a formula anymore than what I've done in the past has been, because I'm not a formula. I worked very hard in my Rancho Mirage house to take the desert colors and shapes and hard regional materials and make a warm house. Yet, now it's time for me to move on and soften the edges, not necessarily for everyone else, but for me. Others will perhaps still want a home like my Rancho Mirage home because this will be different for them. But, I've already done this.

Regarding my office, I debated three years with myself whether or not to build it. Sometimes I'm sorry I did, too, because it's an obligation, a mortgage, and, at twelve thousand square feet, bigger than I need. Sixteen people occupying more than six hundred square feet per person. But, I do like the fact that everyone has his or her own private office rather than a cubicle, plus a wonderful kitchen and a sample room.

In addition, it's helpful to have a showcase of your work. Most people who come to Steve Chase Associates are familiar with what we've done. But some aren't, and the office, like the house, enables them to understand what we can accomplish. If you're working out of your garage, they can't necessarily tell. On the other hand, if you're a one or two person firm and only taking on two jobs a year, you don't need to have all these obligations I have. And, I am trying to cut back. I would like to work only three or four days a week and travel more, and I fully intend to do this. But by the time I do, I want to enable my five key people to take over the company. I'm trying to expose them now, and when I do cut back on my own involvement, the large space will probably seem even more worthwhile, because it will give them a chance to expand.

However, the real value of good design results not from the size of a space but how that space is handled so it truly serves the user's needs. For example, I recently was asked to visit the home of a woman who had done it herself. There was nothing wrong with her home...at least the taste wasn't bad. But the problem was that nothing worked. She doesn't have storage in her nightstands. She hasn't selected furnishings that cooperate with the architecture. And now, though she doesn't know exactly why, she's somewhat uncomfortable with the results. And, these are aspects that a designer could have handled easily in the first place. It's not just a case of choosing the most elegant chintz. As a designer, I make a room work...for people.

top

Master Bath.

bottom left

Master Bedroom.

bottom right

Dining Room.

Photography by Arthur Coleman

Photography by Arthur Coleman

Photography by Arthur Coleman

Photography by Lynn Lown

James Jereb

at home

Photography by Carla Breeze

top

Everything I design I execute with my own hands. That's part of the power.

opposite

If not making something, I'm always writing. One project is a book which will accompany the traveling exhibition of the collection based on my some thirty to forty trips to the Berber tribes of North Africa.

Photography by Carla Breeze

The important thing is not just to see...but to feel.

That's the reason my home of necessity is my studio—except for when I am working on site, which is often, since I am a designer and builder of walls. Other than that, my home is my studio because there's no other way. You can't just walk away from design. At least I can't. I look at living life as an art form.

My sole purpose and theme is to incorporate the North African and Sub-Saharan traditions of architecture and decoration with the Southwest Native American and Colonial traditions. My design reflects a reemergence of these traditions coupled with the design and motifs that exude power and aesthetics from the divine creative source. I believe I am disseminating understanding of symbols and motifs of universal tribal belief systems and that these need to be incorporated into the design of our living environments, private as well as public.

I live in a one hundred fifty-year-old adobe six blocks from the center of Santa Fe, New Mexico. I am continually reworking it to include these universal symbols. For example, I recently created a turtle in bas-relief on an exterior second floor wall as a tribute to Earth Mother. It's covered with Antonio Gaudi-ish tile mosaics with a sacred spiral of mirror placed down the turtle's center. Such an animal in bas-relief is very African and steeped in cultural belief.

Now, in the deepest sense, the cultural meaning of that turtle is not just African but universal. I see no reason not to mix tribal designs from throughout the world. I have now created at my own home archways and walkways that are Spanish...a different color on every wall, each hue derived from one of the several hundred Berber tribes in North Africa, many of which I have visited...adobe fireplaces, raised beds, niches and even an altar inset with tile, glass and pottery shards, all of which also are North African in feeling.

As I look at the project in a holistic sense, I incorporate such elements as these outside as well as inside. Like the ancients, I believe that the interior, exterior and landscaping must all go together to form a spiritual and spatial whole.

My area of expertise academically is African and New Guinean art and, wherever I am, doing whatever project,

my work is the application of all the ideas I've ever absorbed. So, every year as I get more clarity, my environment has to change with me. The bottom line for everything I do is spiritual.

Tribal Design Studios has to do with tribal design from all over the world, and this becomes the collective unconscious. However, I do believe that Native American symbology is particularly important for people in the United States to appreciate. It's right in our own backyard, yet we have the tendency to revere all the exotics and forget about the heritage of our own land.

Throughout my design, there is a recognition of spiritual consciousness. For example, the reason I use many animal forms is that I believe in animal medicine, in the power of animals. Relief figures created with this belief and not purely for decoration not only represent but also exude power. I believe we need more such connections with Earth Mother and her animals. Our being out of touch with nature is one reason our planet is in its impoverished state today.

Not one item in my house, not one aspect, is created for whimsy, even though the result often delights the eye. For me it is my spiritual belief which is the basis of my work. I do not make things for display. I am an educator by background, and it's in my character to communicate ideas. But first of all, my work stems from my own deep inner belief. I am not just performing for others, and I think people who see my home understand that, if only subliminally.

Living in Santa Fe surrounds me with the genre to nurture my art and to support it visually and through cultural context. But, design and color can be approached with the same intuitive feeling for their healing and powerful aspects no matter where one lives. For example, I started my career by painting Victorian houses in Chicago, signing my buildings as I sign each of my walls today, with much joy in my sense of accomplishment. Even there in such a different setting, I realized I was dealing with design and color in a deeply positive way. I wasn't just decorating. I was given the opportunity and the ability to redirect entire neighborhoods, to change and improve people's lives.

Photography by Carla Breeze

opposite

Doors are mystical. I designed, built and painted this one.

top left

I combine Berber textiles with old African mud cloth and Oriental pieces...until I feel like Matisse!

top right

My fireplace blends Southwestern symbols with Berber tattoos and tribal symbols, which really are very similar to those of North American tribes. The two scorpions in bas-relief are symbols of creativity exuding power and magic.

bottom left

The old cupboard in my bedroom is as relaxed as the look of the clothes I design for myself, then have made from the tribal textiles I collect.

bottom right

This is my style of eclectic: tile from Morocco, Berber pots and artifacts, and Arts and Crafts desk and lamp, all set against a North African vernacular blue and punctuated with a very Georgia O'Keeffe cow skull.

Paul Draper
at home

All photography by Klein+Wilson

E very interior space, and every detail within it, must have a distinct personality. It must have character. It must have a life of its own. In terms of a home, it needs to reflect the people who live there. That is why this home reflects not so much the look I have created for other clients, or even our city of Dallas but, for me and my family, our interests and travels.

Without its relationship to the people who live there, a space cannot feel alive. More than anything else, I strive to avoid the feeling that everything is inaccessible, cut off by those psychological ropes that would separate history from today, or beauty and art from comfort and warmth.

Although my work does not imitate their specific styles, I have been most deeply influenced by certain architects of the twentieth century: Aero Saarinen for realizing that each project should have its own individual solution rather than one derived from the designer's own preconceptions; Mies Van der Rohe for emphasizing that form must follow function—although too often this idea is followed without attending to the individual user's psychological needs; and Frank Lloyd Wright for insisting on the integration of landscape, architecture and interiors. These lessons influence me in all my work and nowhere more significantly than in the environment I have created at home.

My life experiences have buoyed this train of thought. For example, when I lived and worked in Asia, I became deeply conscious that there is more than one solution for everything...the use of chopsticks instead of Western flatware, for example. Also, the opportunity to travel and collect art has extended my understanding of what is special and made from the heart and what has been made with a somewhat cookie-cutter approach and lacks feeling and individuality.

Gaining a perspective on what it is we as designers are really doing is, as far as I am concerned, the most important part of my work, and it is not a part that can be left at the office. Sometimes my best thinking, my best design work, occurs at three o'clock in the morning. That is the reason it became important to have my design studio at my home. The office of Paul Draper and Associates is just ten minutes away, but for seventy-five percent of the time, my own work...and my best work...is done here, surrounded by that environment that has life and meaning for me.

top

Having my design studio filled with some of my favorite pieces from my collection provides me with a creatively stimulating environment, which is at the same time personally warm and comfortable. Surrounding me here is an eighteenth-century Korean painting of a tiger, a seventeenth-century pair of Japanese guardian lions and a Ching Dynasty Chinese desk of elm wood.

bottom left

The passage from our house to my studio...a constant reminder to maintain a sense of serenity, both in life and in work.

bottom right

I believe that the careful juxtaposition of different artistic styles can offer new insights into the beauty within each object of art that would be lost if viewed alone. In this corner of our living room, a Ming dynasty painting on silk of gibbons playing in the trees hangs over a contemporary demi-lune table by California artisan C. S. Welch. Atop the table sits an early Roman vase, a small verdigris Chinese chariot fitting dating to the first century B.C., and a bamboo cane topped with a monkey holding his head, from nineteenth-century England.

top

Since I was nine years old, I have been collecting spirited treasures from different cultures. Here, in this view of our living room looking toward the dining room, is part of our varied collection: the dining room lamp by Ingo Maurer of Japanese handmade paper; behind it on the right, a mezzotint by the contemporary Japanese artist T. Yakoi, and to the left of the mezzotint, a Japanese *noren* hangs at the entry to the library. The dining chairs are from Michael Taylor, while the table itself is an eighteenth-century English library table. Against the far wall in the dining room is an antique Korean "scholar's chest." In the foreground is an Edo period Japanese mask and a large eighteenth-century Chinese ink painting of mythical beasts. Living with this art is a daily reminder of special memories and travels associated with collecting.

bottom

In selecting pieces of art, I look for those that have inner life, and for my own collection I love certain representations of animals and mythological beasts. In the foreground an antique Japanese tiger overlooks a favorite Anglo-Indian chair. Next to the fireplace, a seventeenth-century Zen painting depicts a monkey foolishly trying to catch the moon's reflection in the water below. On the table sits a fossilized crab, one of my favorite pieces. It is estimated to be forty million years old, and the New York archaeological shop in which I found it had whimsically named it the "dancing crab."

Photography by Horst Neumann and Juliana Balint Production

Dennis Jenkins
at home

Photography by © Steven Brooke

opposite

In the library, I placed a hand-carved piece of stone in the middle of the tile wall above the tub, my symbol of early samples of learning and writing found along the Euphrates. The tub is a great place to sit and read. I also like its 1900 form in juxtaposition with the table in the foreground by Miami architect Robert Whitton.

top left

When Sunny and I began our work on Villa Malaga, our hope was that, when we were done, we would be *home* in the strongest sense of the word.

top right

For the front court, we set Florida key stone in a bed of sand…a natural, practical solution considering the amount of rain here.

bottom left

"Sotto Voce," soft voice, really says it all. At Villa Malaga nothing seems overpowering, but everything seems to speak softly…even the walls.

bottom right

In the entry foyer, I carved, scraped and stippled until the new plaster wall looked as if it might be five thousand years old. To us it represents the layers and layers of human activity that happen over time. We liked the effect so much we continued the process into what had been an adjacent telephone booth and linen closet.

The place was a wreck. Hardly a "villa" in any sense of the word when Sunny McLean and I found it in 1978. It was in such poor condition, it was suggested by structural engineers that it should be demolished. But we saw beyond that…we saw the promise of a home we could enjoy immensely every day. The house was built in 1926, in Coconut Grove, Florida, and encompasses scarcely more than two thousand square feet. Today it is Villa Malaga, our home and, to us, a place of magic.

Confined within a property of fifty-five feet by one hundred twenty-three feet, the once-existing open court (enclosed by previous remodeling) has been made to function as a classic atrium. This atrium provides a natural central core and transition between all the spaces of the main house which surround it. Each individual space is willfully and decisively shaped to its particular function, discreet yet complementary. Several walls have been removed, other walls thickened and openings made more sensitive to natural ventilation assisted by ceiling fans. Throughout the house, variations of spacings, colors and textures emphasize axes and frame targets of attention while dissolving the fixed vista.

The existing floors are oak, and the walls are five different colors of off-white tinted limestone plaster. The plaster is textured, then sanded to a polished soap-stone smoothness, sealed with oil, waxed and buffed to a satin finish. The doors, trim and ceiling are select vertical grain fir, sanded and sealed with clear Danish oil. The hardware throughout is solid polished brass. Tile is used extensively in both traditional and non-traditional applications. Mexican Cantera stone, handmade cement Astra tile and handpainted ceramic tile from throughout the world—much of it available through Sunny's tile and bath fixtures showrooms—can be found in every room.

We did one room at a time… slowly…and that was what allowed the design to develop into a haven of casual privacy, illusion and indulgence. There is a lot of experimentation here, and the serendipity that comes from trial and error. Often what some people would see as mistakes actually lend charm to a place, the type of charm that allows you to feel superior rather than inferior to a structu   Massive planes and complete perfection are not humane enough for the two of us. But, here, we come home and feel as if we want to hug our house. It has such a simpleness about it, even though it was accomplished by some rather sophisticated techniques. It truly represents an evolution for me, and it never could have happened without Sunny. She is much more flexible than I, who was trained as a Modernist. Through her I learned to deal with things in a more casual manner, and to allow a concept so conducive to personal choice to evolve. Through a multiplicity of forms and organic textures that meld our aesthetic, emotional and intellectual preferences, our home today provides us continually with an ongoing source of inspiration.

Photography by © Steven Brooke

Photography by Horst Neumann and Juliana Balint Production

Photography by Horst Neumann and Juliana Balint Production

top

The explosion of purple in the patio startles some people…they say it's not a tropical color…but to me it is at once sensual, tropical and royal, and absolutely right in that location.

bottom

There is a primal expression in the serpentine form of our wall, but it also performs a function. Its height begins at seventeen inches, or seat height, which is good for entertaining, and ends here as a six-foot backdrop behind more traditional furniture.

top left

In the atrium/living area, we installed a wall of copper-glazed tile from Sunny McLean & Co. that has an almost fish scale iridescence. It and everything in the room, eclectic as it is, reflect our intense belief in regionalism.

top right

In the master bedroom, Miami artist Ellen Moss rendered our ideas of tropical symbolism with benevolent Haitian voodoo symbols.

bottom left

In the atrium, more layering and stippling seems to set one free from the passage of time.

bottom right

We collected bits of tile for six years, then looked at the spaces between the trees, then started building…

Kenneth Ko

at work & at home

Photography courtesy of
Capital Magazine (Stephen Ng)

I am proud of my heritage and would like nothing better than to feel my work has successfully blended Chinese architectural concepts with modern technology and Western comfort. So, this is what I have tried to do in my own home and office.

Kenneth Ko Designs occupies the top three floors of an industrial building in Hong Kong. It is located in Shatin, the New Territories, a little distance out of the commercial center, in an industrial area.

I enjoy the contrast of having my office in such a utilitarian building and have created the feeling here of an oasis in the midst of its quite undesigned surroundings.

Unlike standard office space with its low false ceiling grids and claustrophobic feeling, the industrial accommodation has lofty ceilings, giving spaciousness and light to the office. The atmosphere is somewhat reminiscent of a New York warehouse. It is an internalized environment, with its own picturesque rooftop garden.

To give character and warmth to the setting, I have employed heavily textured materials—railroad ties, painted steel girders, unpolished granite floors and rough terra cotta tiles. Even the steps are tree stumps. Contrasting with this rough-hewn look are elements of a completely different sort, such as antique chandeliers, inlaid marble, and finely painted and sculpted works of art.

The office is open in plan, as I believe this is more conducive to a creative interchange of ideas among the design staff. It also maintains a feeling of spaciousness, very important in such a crowded metropolis as Hong Kong. My own work space is situated on a raised platform in the center, enabling me to be in touch with everything going on in the entire office.

As I enjoy simplicity and clean lines, the office walls and ceiling are all painted white. Adding warmth and individuality to the setting are the many handcrafted and textured accessories and architectural elements I am always collecting from my travels abroad. Frequently, these include visits to Turkey, Morocco, India, Pakistan and Thailand where the arts of craftsmen still live on, and I bring examples of their work home to stimulate my own imagination and hopefully that of my clients as well. Since these acquisitions often become part of various projects' artistic

palettes, the specific atmosphere of my office is always changing, always ready for more provocative additions from abroad.

My home is a rural property near Kam Tin Village in Hong Kong's New Territories. This is like a rural retreat, suited to my living requirements of casual comfort.

The main section is an original one-room village house common to Hong Kong villages, and it is flanked by two wings added in recent times. Since I wanted to retain the original structure and character of the village house, I have left the beams exposed and stained them a dark brown to contrast with the natural color of the Peking roof tiles. The rustic theme is extended to terra cotta Canton floor tiles.

The existing divider walls I demolished to make room for an open-planned kitchen. Industrial piping forms a bold exhaust hood over the stove. Elsewhere, handcrafted items continue to bring the warmth and individuality I like in all my surroundings. Even outside, a garden of fruit trees and bougainvillea enclosed by a red brick wall continues the blend of rustic charm and urban comfort.

The rooms of my house have picture windows, framing various views of the garden, which is dramatically illuminated at night. Taking advantage of this lush perspective is the bathroom, as well as my private gym. Fitness and peak physical condition are of great significance to me; I work out every day.

Another bathroom is located outdoors, in the garden. Completely open to its surroundings, toilet and all, it enables one to gaze at all the trees and flowers and out to the paddy fields beyond.

Such living experiences are, in the end, what design is all about. People, not books, are the basis of architecture. You have to know and understand people before you can design buildings for them.

When I work for other people, I find out everything I can about them—their habits, what colors they like, their tastes, their lifestyles. It is a bit like being a psychologist. A designer must have a high standard of appreciation, be totally open to accept people's ideas, be able to communicate with clients on a one-to-one level. The designer must be easy to talk to and always eager to learn from others' needs and requirements.

When you design for yourself, many of the same rules apply. You really have to know yourself, your lifestyle, and how you want to live—because the architecture and design that surround you will influence every day of your life. So, while I enjoy everything I am asked to create for clients, I have found that, for my own environment, I prefer emphasizing my own background. I have learned I am happiest with a home and office that incorporate great comfort and current technology, yet emanate an attitude that is strongly Chinese.

top

Even in my conference room, I surround myself with the handcrafted items from my collection. Behind is inlaid marble from India. I made the table from a partition from an old Chinese house.

top

Our staff cantina.

left

At Kenneth Ko Designs Ltd., we display our extensive stock of accessories and architectural elements throughout to broaden our artistic palette for various projects with which we are involved. Of course, this means that our office environment is continually changing. Perhaps that is a special luxury of the interior designer. To be able to buy and sell beautiful items from all over the world enables us to bring much vitality to our personal surroundings. It is never boring, always lively.

right

Living room, first floor.

bottom

Swimming pool under glass-walled dining room.

top

My home in the Yuen Long area of Hong Kong has been the backdrop for many movies during the past ten years. When I have dinner, the pool is illuminated, making the house seem to float, mysterious and dream-like, on the glowing, still, blue water.

left

Master bedroom, second floor.

Donald Maxcy
at work & at home

My wife Marsha and I have been working together as a design team for the past eleven years, from a tiny studio in our home (the lighting for the Monterey Bay Aquarium was designed from this space) until the firm grew into its present location in downtown Monterey, California.

Our interior design practice began in San Francisco, spread into the Santa Clara Valley, and from the Monterey Peninsula mushroomed across the country. I myself am a graduate of the Rudolph Schaeffer School of Design in San Francisco and have a background in fine arts, theater and film. I did not tap into architectural lighting as part of my practice...it was purely out of necessity. The light color rendition often ruined a carefully selected color scheme or distracted from the dramatic quality of the interior spaces I had designed.

I suppose I have always "seen" light differently. I see the magic and drama of shadow patterns. I see how lighting affects people's moods and creates a special sense of place. In order to make this happen for our clients, I use a great deal of intuition mixed with serious technical knowledge. We approach our practice of lighting as an art form rather than an engineering necessity. We like to think of our design practice as unique, not only because each client is different with each project reflecting his or her individuality, but also because of the close attention we give to textures and detail with the added element of lighting.

This takes a great deal of energy as we work with each of our clients as if his or hers was our only project, especially since our clients are widespread. Currently we have projects in New York City, Livingston (New Jersey), Pebble Beach, Virginia Beach (Virginia), Telegraph Hill in San Francisco as well as a church across the Bay, one of the homes which burned in the 1991 Oakland fire, and several more north and south of here, all in various stages of activity. The part you never hear about is when we have to run and catch

top right

With its monochromatic grey palette, the enclosed conference room is also the site of lighting demonstrations for the firm's clients. Lighting is best understood and appreciated through hands-on experience. The platform with pillows is for the principal who, because of a back disability, must sometimes work in a reclining position. The brush and ink work on Japanese paper is by Richard Dunning.

bottom

The mirror effect above the slot wall in the entry to our office suggests infinite space. A Henry Esparza *Lotus Dance* collage hangs in the reception area to welcome visitors. The wine-colored slot wall material was selected in a reflective material so it would allow return light into the space even though it is a dark value.

left

In our living room, the eighty-four-inch by forty-eight-inch oil mixed media on canvas is by Michael Brangoccio entitled *Announcement*. We were immediately attracted to Michael's work because of his use of raw materials and Asian elements. There is a second piece of his on the far side of the fireplace, a thirty-inch by twenty-two-inch mixed media collage on paper.

bottom

The intricately detailed hanging tapestry in the bedroom is from Thailand. It is hand-woven and embroidered, showing temple dancers in gold threads and crystal beads and takes candlelight beautifully.

a plane to a job site, work fourteen to twenty hours, and are expected to appear at a press party or opening reception looking as if we have been on the golf course all day, when in fact we have not been eating right or sleeping...does this sound familiar?

Our office environment was carefully designed to function as a work space, as well as provide the lighting effects most difficult to describe to clients and to make a design statement about who we are. For us, this is best achieved through a minimalist approach, simple lines and a hierarchy of texture and finishes.

Our work space is better suited for a bowling alley because the main office space is sixteen feet by sixty-four feet. We have room for a five person staff and the office allows us to communicate easily across the office partitions. The design business is sharing people's best creative ideas and getting the work stated in an interpretable manner. Our office lends itself to this creative process.

The lighting aspect of our work is very copious and detailed, because we put lighting in unconventional places and use the fixturing differently, often customizing or adapting. Right now we are about to issue quarter-inch scale plans entailing five oversized sheets of layout, wiring and details of exactly how and where to install the fixture architecturally in addition to a cutbook of each and every fixture on the job, its finish, wattage load and lamping specs. After installation of fixturing and furnishings, we return to the job and focus the lighting (performed at night), adding custom lenses and accessories, and calibrating the computer controls with the client.

The interior aspect of our work is equally complex. Our designs are so comfortable and thought-out with an enormous sense of detail that it is often very architectural. For example, our

work on the Laurel Birch Gallerie in Carmel, only two thousand square feet of space, was generated on thirteen enormous pages of quarter-inch scale detailing regarding what lighting was to be used and how it was to be installed. We showed how mirrors were to be integrated into the cabinets, how a carpet border was to be installed up the stairs, where the store was to lay out certain display merchandise, how the store's display designer could "build" up stone blocks into various display shapes and forms. Our plans are detailed enough to be used for bidding, as a planning tool for the client, or as an installation tool for the contractors. The interior plans can be as complex as our lighting plans, although you wouldn't think it to be true or necessary.

Because our work involves such complexity and discipline, our home environment contains elements we find appealing emotionally, as well as aesthetically. By the time we reach our front gate at the end of the day or on the weekend, we virtually lock out the world in order to re-charge and relax. Our home is in total contrast to the highly intricate world of our business. It is a very small cottage, located in a forest of oaks and pines atop a hill in Monterey, reminiscent of Carmel, and often cloaked in a mystical fog further rendering a "quietness" similar to an oriental landscape. We share our home with our dog Sandy, an orange cat Leonardo, and a brilliant blue/green parrot Sasha. Sandy and Sasha can often be found at the office as well as at home.

Because we both relate to organic and natural forms and enjoy being outside, we go mountain hiking and camping (to get us back to the basics). An important part of our home environment is tending the drycreek stream bed and black bamboo garden we have

acquired during the past twenty-one years of our marriage. The house structure itself is full of irregularities which we fondly call "primitive." It is a one-story, two-bedroom, two-bath redwood frame in odd angles with floor-to-ceiling glass panels which further allow us to enjoy the surrounding forest.

What lies ahead for us? New challenges such as designing light fixtures and furniture and adopting new members into our family of clients. Further refining and defining very personal and unusual solutions for our designs and delving into what this experience of life is all about—that's our plan.

My credo is...food, love and art...in any combination.

Alie Chang
Paul

at home

All photography by Mary E. Nichols Photography

My father was a practicing architect in Shanghai, China, prior to 1948. He greatly influenced my philosophy of home design and building. One of the ancient practices in Old China was the study of *Feng Shui* which is the evaluation of the building structure in relationship with the earth, geology, as well as sun, moon and stars orientation. I tried to incorporate my innate sense of Feng Shui philosophy into my home, as I do in all my designs, so that the house would be harmonious with the land in which it is rooted.

I completed five years' formal training in art and design education in Taipei. There I learned under contemporary masters in Chinese calligraphy about the way ancient Chinese ink painters dealt with abstract philosophical spaces. I learned to look at humanity as an integral part of nature and nature as a force in our everyday life. I also received extensive Western art training in oil painting and watercolor, sculpture, material usage and human anatomy. All of these disciplines are part of my design process. I look at a home or building as if it is a hollow sculpture. Its function is the part of space that is empty. The Zen philosophy teaches me peace of mind and is achieved by following the flow of nature's energy. Therefore, in approaching the design, I start with an inner process rather than with the imposition of a style or a method of construction.

My husband Phil, with his European origin, also added another dimension to my design. We both wanted a home that would give us a sense of freedom and fun; a place to reflect, to work, and most importantly a place to share with family and friends. We built our special "Feng Shui Garden House" facing the Santa Monica Canyon. Hugging a lush hillside, the five thousand-five hundred square foot house is actually a stone and wood structure that blends into its natural surroundings.

Planned "zones" in each of the house's multi-levels provide ample space for leisure activities. These spaces include an audio-visual entertainment center, gardening center and an open air art studio located on the rooftop surrounded by canyon greenery and distant ocean views and meditation spots. Other personalized areas include a sunny window seat for catnapping or reading, an underground passageway leading to a vaulted wine cellar, an exercise/massage room off the master bedroom, an office/study that can be reached by crossing the stepping stones over a fish pond, small guest quarters, an artist's studio with steps leading to the open-air rooftop and a complete living suite with a separate entrance which our daughter, Angi, uses when she visits from college. We enjoy entertaining outdoors, so we included an outdoor dining area.

No matter where we are, inside or outside, we can always hear distant ocean waves and canyon activity, such as a bird family taking up residence in a nearby tree, a squirrel searching for food, or a raccoon family sneaking a midnight drink from our master bath fountain. The sound of water and nature is one of the reasons why we built our home here, and why we added the fern grotto and waterfall in the foyer. The grotto has a nine-year-old turtle as a resident and he co-habits with a colony of Koi fish. Our need to be surrounded by natural sounds is also reflected in our master bath, an *adoquin* stone fountain against a mural landscape by myself with the help of my artist sister, Lilee Chang Ma, and a terra cotta "fishman" fountain in the sculpture garden. Water sounds make the picture complete, replacing the missing pebbled creek that was once located just one hundred feet from our home.

Besides aesthetic and philosophical considerations, environmental safety in a home is a very important issue to me. It is critical to check the safety of a building's structural or furnishing materials, such as insulation or fabric contents, for elements or chemicals that are hazardous to one's health. Due to the availability of high technology today, the area of electrical and magnetic field penetration is of great concern. I have extensive exposure in this field of knowledge and my design firm makes sure that the houses we build are organically oriented, utilizing natural life sources, cross air ventilation, and natural materials for interior furnishings. In addition to passive cooling and heating built-in features, a radiant heating system was added to provide extra comfort when walking barefoot on the limestone floor. For example, the waterfall in our home acts as a natural humidifier, and the indoor plants are a natural air purifier.

While I find it important to consider home furnishings that contribute to one's physical well-being, consideration is also given to mental health as well. A home is a refuge from a chaotic world, and to me the most challenging part of a design is to create a unique and distinct image that reflects the owners' philosophy of life. Sometimes, a great deal of soul-searching is necessary to discover one's hidden psychological needs, perhaps recalling some fond childhood memories, or a long forgotten fantasy of an ultimate dream.

I believe each home should have its own mystique. It should reflect something in one's past, one's present, and project in some way one's future. As one moves between spaces, the interest should unfold and from time to time offer surprising elements, whether an unexpected view...a meditation garden with an open bath...or a secluded balcony. I often witness my clients evolve from one stage of life to one totally different, and always better. Sharing and contributing in this growth process gives me untold gratification.

When we moved into our house fifteen years ago, our daughter Angi was just five years old. Now that she is away at college, Phil's physical needs and my own have changed. However, the house was designed to easily accommodate these changes. The Feng Shui and Zen philosophies have taken care of that, while the latest technology provides us with a home in which to grow, evolve and move forward.

top left

This is my office, which allows me to separate my work area from the conference area (at the end of the stepping stone entry at the other side of the house). Here I have a view of the garden and access to the carport and rear entrance.

top right

Our dining room is a true dining area—in fact, there are two, one indoor and one outdoor. It is a place we can enjoy good food and enrichment for body and soul.

opposite

This is the staircase leading to the master bedroom and exercise room. It has an elongated skylight that is three feet by eighteen feet. The staircase creates a triangular space, a sculptured space that is narrower at the bottom than at top, and which reminds one that a house is a hollow sculpture created with positive and negative spaces to make it special.

After a brief flight of stairs, guests arrive at this alcove garden area with sunlight filtering through the jacaranda tree and layers of ferns and tropical plants. My sister Lilee Chang Ma is an artist and she and I created a large wall mural to add depth and fantasy.

top

After they enter the house, guests find a fern grotto with waterfall and Koi fishpond, where my nine-year-old water turtle resides. A skylight two-stories above filters down sunlight to allow the orchids and other exotic plants to flourish. Stepping stones leading to my conference room enable clients to enter directly from the outdoors.

bottom left

At the landing in the middle of the staircase we have cantilevered an area so we have a nook for reading.

bottom right

The master bath has a steam bath and spa tub; the glass blocks provide privacy and light; the window insert allows a spectacular canyon view.

The living room is the place where we gather with friends and enjoy conversation. The colors are the same muted, multi-hued compositions that one sees in each room, interrelated but varying slightly from one room to another to add additional interest. These colors give one the warmth of the earth and the feel of sunlight that filters through every part of the house, providing the calmness and tranquility that I wish to emphasize.

Clodagh

at home

I live in a New York loft with nineteen windows. It's all open and translucent. The walls are stripped brick with the residue of white paint deliberately left on to give a feeling of patination. The ceilings are continuous brick barrel vaults. There is a wood-burning stove, an open kitchen with cabinets made of amber washed ash. The counters are khaki concrete, poured into an edging of patinated steel. There are herbs and ivies in window boxes. I have two large friendly dogs. When I walk in, I feel that I am at home in the country although I can see the Empire State Building out of the windows. The doors to each room are shoji and so translucent that at night the light flows through and they look like giant lanterns.

I feel strongly about where we all spend our time. I am lucky; my commute from my office is a flight of stairs. Too many people have no choice but to drive to their office at dawn, spending months of their lives in their cars. Life should be more than a series of Styrofoam cups. We live where we work and we work where we live.

When I started out in my own fashion business in Ireland I was seventeen and had a lovely brick Georgian house. That open house feeling worked very well. My clients used to come to afternoon tea and try on fashions and discuss style. However, my office was a fifteen minute drive from my home, doubled or more in rush hour, and I lived with a constant pull to be where I was not. Now, I can invite my staff and clients upstairs for tea and continue discussions in comfort until all hours. I love to cook and think it's good to integrate that with being together. It's part of enjoying life. I often have a working lunch with my partner Robert Pierpont.

Our office downstairs is very informal, more like a studio where we can model build without restraints. We make full scale studies of our furniture and lighting so that we can detect problems before a piece is finalized. We also make study models of the spaces we design so that we can study the flow of a space more accurately. Most clients enjoy this process more than studying plans and elevations, as it is more easily understandable.

I can invite new clients in, let them look at work in progress, then bring them upstairs, let them walk around and look at the materials and furniture I've selected for myself. It gives them a glimpse into who I am and it cements the relationship that must exist between designer and client. Designers can be intimidating and I ask very personal questions of my clients, yet by exposing myself, they will feel comfortable enough to do the same.

This is also why I only use my first name. My parents felt that you had to know people twenty years before you could use their first names. I think being called by one's first name is preferable whether a person is the President or a charlady. There is no savings account for love and friendship or the type of intimate conversation you can share with people when you know them better. Clients feel comfortable telling me what I need to know: who they are, their wish list, if they want to go barefoot, who sleeps on which side of the bed, how they like their offices and showrooms to work, what will reinforce their persona in the work environment, how they view their corporate image.

This I think is my value for clients. I change their perception of designers as decorators. I look at us as travel guides to a new type of lifestyle, specialists who can design the irritations out of other people's lives. *Feng Shui,* the Chinese art and science of place-making, is a continuing thread in my work. It, too, like design, is a healing art, a life enhancing art. It increases the flow of energy so you can avoid stagnation. A house is like a body through which blood has to flow quickly to maintain health. Sarah Rossbach is our Feng Shui consultant and we use her advice and guidance on all our projects.

One question I continually ask myself is "Am I doing this because I want to or because I'm expected to?" I ask the same of clients "Am I bulldozing you?" As I grow, I am less influenced by social structure, yet there are certain infrastructures in a family one must, as a designer, be aware of. I study people, the way they live and work and I and

top

With my partner, the architect Robert Pierpont, testing one of my new vegetarian recipes.

my husband (architectural and travel photographer Daniel Aubry) and my children, though they're grown up now, have been my guinea pigs.

A sense of grounding is so important. I like to give a feeling of being in touch with the earth through my use of materials and textures, especially in high-rises. I use low maintenance materials. I erode and sponge them so they can only get more beautiful as they get older. I also do a lot of research on environmentally correct products. I sandblast woods and dislike double waxed finishes along with all-white carpets and sofas. It's all so crisp and pure that you wind up being the only imperfect thing there.

On the other hand, you are comfortable in the country where stains don't pop out at you. So, I use a lot of flamed and natural cleft stone, textured walls and lots of plaster and joint compound to give a permanent feeling. I use generic fabrics that don't look overly designed and do look as if they've been around for some time. I like something to look as if it's the one thing I haven't touched...when in fact I have.

I create spaces where people can actualize themselves. Clients write, after I've completed their home or office, that their place is peaceful or that I've enhanced their lives. They rarely write about what I've designed. That's when I know I've achieved my goal: that my design has healed.

All photography by Daniel Aubry

The all cotton king-sized futon is opposite the whirlpool bath. The bed is slightly raised on a platform. The mirror is an integral element of Feng Shui.

top left

Counter detail of ground
steel.

top right

Overall view of the
kitchen, gallery beyond,
and Duke.

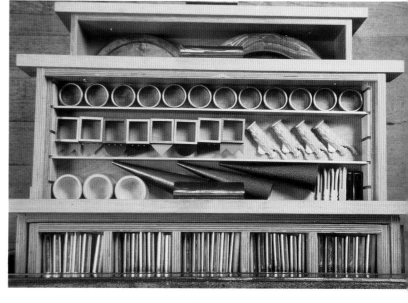

top left

Inside door storage is held in place with coiled spring bar.

top right

More storage utilization.

bottom left

Slots guide knife for easy cutting.

bottom right

Drawer with custom dividers, designed to specifically fit the flatware and such.

All photography by John Vaughan

Thomas Bartlett
at work & at home

When I was a student at California College of Arts and Crafts, and still later when I was a tour guide at Hearst Castle before returning to my native Napa Valley, I debated whether I should be a painter or an interior designer. The latter won out, and I soon established my own firm in nearby Yountville, California, in 1969.

Today, I have clients all over the country, from banks to boutiques to restaurants. And now that I am established in St. Helena amid the California wine country, I have a fine showroom as well, and I conduct my design business from there.

I have always done a lot of projects in the country house look that I like for myself, both at work and at home, be it my house in Napa Valley or even in my pied-á-terre in San Francisco, which is just an hour away. However, I am truly interested in each client and what he or she wants. I consider that what I bring to the client are the tools to express another person's dreams and answer another person's needs. So, I have done some very contemporary spaces as well as some that appear to be in such distress that you would have thought them untouched for the last two hundred years.

Mainly, as a creative person, I am always looking for that twist by which I can answer the client's specific needs and also do something challenging, something unlike anything I've ever done before. I have seven full-time people on staff including two design associates to assist me in this. It is not play—even though I like what I do so much that it doesn't seem like work.

That is probably why my office is open seven days a week—my office being a corner in my showroom from which I can seek privacy but always maintain an overview of what's going on. The people who come there are often new clients, but often they're old ones, and now just as much friends as clients. My life is a whole. This is where I started. My parents live nearby and my two Persian cats, Norma and J.C., are named after them. I like my life.

I do try to leave about every three months for seven to ten days to relax. And, once a year I go on a buying trip to Europe, twice a year to New York. This is important not just for business but for recharging the batteries.

My style may often be Country, but I am not interested in being stylish or cute but in really helping other people improve their lives. If I can help them live with honesty, comfort and beauty—and perhaps above all in this time when most people don't have a staff, with a place that functions, that really serves them in conducting their lives—then I am satisfied.

For my personal surroundings, what I seek most of all, what I consider most beautiful, is a sense of serenity. I feel best with muted colors, solitude and peace. I don't own a television set and I don't even turn on music. But, I love to hear the rain. I am drawn outside by the songs of birds. And I do love the company of those cats and my thirteen-year-old apricot schipperke.

I am still painting and drawing a little, and when I do I am reminded of all the beautiful things I have seen at some of my favorite museums, such as the Uffizi in Florence and the Vatican Museum in Rome. And, I cannot help but draw a parallel between the revelations of peace, beauty and comfort by those past great masters, and what we as professional interior designers are trying to bring into people's lives today.

top left

Clients Jerry and K. C. Cunningham, on my right and left, saw this blue-and-white Royal Copenhagen charger and purchased an entire set that very day.

top right

The studio for me is like a laboratory where I can mix my latest acquisitions and change at will. It also provides an opportunity for clients to see the results of recent trips. Here in my entrance courtyard are some fairly large pots I brought home from Imprenetta in Tuscany outside Florence. The iron furniture is from The Thomas Bartlett Collection which I used to manufacture in Napa Valley but now am having made in the Philippines.

top

The noted California painter Arne Nybak's *Blue Niche with Vegetables and Fruit* (1975) is joined by numerous accessories I've picked up around the world. A real eclecticism cannot be out of a book. It just develops as one collects, then edits, then collects some more.

left

Faux painter Jerry Worman glazed the walls of my showroom/studio three shades of yellow, then I ensconced the two eighteenth-century Chinese wallpaper panels in faux marbre. The armoire I brought back from France. The rabbits, which I represent exclusively, are by California sculptor Burt Kessenick.

In my apartment in San Francisco, there is room on the terrace for an intimate grouping of some pieces from The Thomas Bartlett Collection in a verdigris finish.

top left

The salon in beiges was designed around my own painting entitled *Landscape*. Some favorite treasures rest on a granite, glass and steel table. The rug is imported coir.

bottom left

A small alcove off the living room has its tables piled high with books for research or just relaxation. An antique stone capital serves as the base for the table which is dominated by a pair of American nineteenth-century etched glass hurricane shades and obelisks by the San Francisco artist, Brett Landenberger.

right

The bedroom is done in Fortuny fabric with Italian bed linens. The lamps were made expressly for me in Murano, Italy. Noted American artist, Paul Cadmus, did the drawing.

Vicente Navarro

at work & at home

The subject of the home and interior design today requires a much broader approach than in the past.

A living space is not defined by mere decoration. When I first start to design a space, I try not to think of end results that come about through concrete solutions whose sole purpose is to beautify. Instead, I attempt to rethink what will be the use and function of the home, to enable my work to be practical. This, of course, influences the aesthetic feeling of everything I design. My work looks as practical as it is.

The most important contribution an interior designer can bring to a project is to always keep in mind the building structure. Not only are the aesthetics important. Also vital are the distribution of the spaces, how they have been envisioned to reflect the true function of a home and the life and work of its inhabitants.

Such a sensitivity toward the actual construction enriches all aspects of a home and provides a unique and individual design much deeper than just superficial decoration.

The correct use of form, and form that is derived directly from the intended use of an object or a space, will always be what is truly beautiful.

My own home in Valencia, Spain, is on the sixth floor of a turn-of-the-century building which had deteriorated due to several remodelings by previous owners. In fact, there was nothing left of the original, so my idea was to create an entirely new look without trying in any way, shape or form to imitate the old look of the house. The floors are wood, the walls are white, and the ceilings are at maximum height. These are the characteristics of the space.

The terrace was designed to look like a patio, and with its marble floors, window detailing and mesh ceiling, it is the only part of the house that is reminiscent of the building's original character.

It is always difficult for an interior designer to do his own home. As a designer, I find that when I am doing my own place, my critical sense doesn't allow my imagination to run wild.

However, maybe that is a good thing. Because as a designer I am surrounded with so many projects and proposals that it is best for my own home to be a refuge from all that. Its being taut, almost antiseptic and definitely not ostentatious, gives my design palette a rest.

Another important aspect of such a minimalist approach is its timelessness. In my studio and showroom, located in the heart of Valencia on Cirilo Amorós, nothing in the basic design has been changed since I did the space in 1980, and yet it does not appear to be dated. You can't tell the passing of time due to the severity of the line and minimal color.

What does change—and changes constantly—is the exhibit of furnishings. Since I distribute Cassina, Acerbis, Molteni, Zanotta, Alivar, Arflex, de Padova, ICF, Flos and Artemide, this is a most important aspect to me.

top left

On my terrace.

top right

My studio and showroom.

bottom

View of the ground floor from the entry.

top

View between floors.

bottom

View from the top of the stairwell.

left

Hallways leading to
bedrooms.

top right

Bedroom.

bottom right

Living Room.

232   at home

bottom

Bathroom.

José Manuel Gomez Vazquez Aldana

at work

S ince 1961, Gomez Vazquez Aldana & Associates has striven to design and create structures which not only perform their function but also delight the eye and are in concert with their environment. For my brother and partner, Jaime Gomez Aldana, and myself it was important to provide our firm and its some eighty professionals with an environment expressive of our goals.

The office has been adapted in the restored building of a gracious old building called "Hacienda," dating from 1904 and located in the Colonia Seattle in Zapopan, Jalisco, Mexico. Originally it was a North American family's residence, but they abandoned it around 1914 because of the Mexican revolution. The area called Colonia Seattle was founded at the turn of the century by Alfred and Virginia (Ninon) Downs who came from the Yukon but were originally from Seattle, Washington. They were looking for new opportunities in mining but, instead, found riches in lands and woods, so they established their home here.

In the 1920s, this house became home to the Hiemer family, and afterwards, in the '40s, was the property of Mr. Carlos Garcia. Later on it was the Ashida family's residence. Finally, in 1974, it became the property of the Gomez Vazquez Aldana family. A beautiful restaurant named La Hacienda de la Flor was established, featuring Mexican food and five-star delicacies. The restaurant was managed by Guillermo Gomez Vazquez Aldana, the older brother of Jaime and me, who was also a Cordon Bleu chef.

In 1990, it was decided to establish this office here, so the remodeling started. The original adobe walls had to be preserved, as did the 1904 wooden stairs and beams. At the same time it was imperative to have the most modern facilities—electricity, audio, plumbing, telephones, communication systems, computers and, above all, functional space planning to house more than one hundred people. The result is a modern, technologically advanced office framed by a turn-of-the-century shady and cool old house.

To us, the beauty of this environment represents something of vital significance. We believe that the built environment, whether office or home or hotel, must not fight with nature but rather go along with nature, give back to nature. If we do that, we will then produce a universe full of positive energy and peace.

We also believe that architecture should be sensual. That does not mean it cannot be technologically advanced, but it must also relate to people's spirit. To do this, architecture and design must consider all five senses—seeing, touching, smelling, hearing and even taste—for people to feel fulfilled. I truly believe that the *Letter of Guadalajara,* written mostly by me, and corrected by Ignacio Díaz Morales and led and supported by I. M. Pei, Philip Johnson, Luis Barragán, Marco Aldaco, Pedro Ramírez Vázquez, Díaz Morales and myself, says it all. This manifesto was signed also by the president of the National Academy of Architecture. The following manifesto includes the reason for the atmosphere we have tried to instill in our office space.

top left

At my own desk, working on the master plan for a major government project in Jalisco. Called Costalegre, it will include an airport, hotels, golf courses, and residential division at its beautiful site on the Pacific.

bottom left

My brother Jaime Gomez Vazquez at his desk.

right

At the entry to our office, the fountain pays homage to nature, without which no architecture or design can be successful no matter what its technological achievement.

From

Manifesto: Carta de Guadalajara. Academia Nacional de Arquitectura de la Sociedad de Arquitectos Mexicanos, A.C., Capitulo Guadalajara. November 1987.

- Architecture, like humanity, throughout the centuries and epochs has different aspects and expressions.
- We shall refer here only to one very important change in this century which has had great influence on the architecture of our times:
- The invaluable contribution of the Bauhaus which broke with the entrenched and effete conventions, and opened again the liberty of man's thinking, an essential premise which permits creativity and ingenuity.
- Even though the Bauhaus established human parameters, for reasons of internal crisis it was unable to mature or transcend to the elevation and well-being of man.
- These circumstances and the eclecticism of the nineteenth century from which we emerged were the causes of the essential disorientation in our theory and "praxis."
- Because of such sequence today, it has produced such disorder and chaos in the majority of today's constructions that it is believed that, by being different, it is good.
- They ignored the environment, urban or natural, using technology as a misguided goal, thus producing a clash between the building and the urban space, the "City,"
- A clash between the particular identity, and community identities, identities which should comply with spatial expressions.
- A depreciation and lack of communication with nature was observed.
- Architecture fell from liberty to disorder.
- There are many more reasons for which current buildings, in the main, are estranged from the essentials and immutables of that which is "Architecture."
- We must recuperate what architecture has been and must be again, if we want man to continue cultivating himself and not become a victim of a consumer society.
- With respect ot the "Human Habitat," we need to restore the essential equilibrium, the scale, order, love, poetry and the lost dialogue with man.
- For this reason, we are obliged to make a serious statement which will emphasize these needs and at the same time enunciate and define what we believe, what we have experienced and what we are.
- That which architecture must be is truly HUMANISTIC, an indispensable characteristic which has for so long been lost.

top left

This is the patio onto which all the architects' and designers' offices look. We wanted to avoid cutting down the tree, so we designed the wall to go all the way around it.

bottom

The difference in the results between a business meeting over luncheon on the terrace by the lily pond and one held inside in a conference room is remarkable.

Rosalind Millstone

A nd so we have heard from classicists, romanticists, explorers and earth spirits...consummate professionals all, but with such different methods and styles. What then is the key element for which they were summoned forth to join each other in this volume?

It is that one absolutely most important element that distinguishes the leading edge in every walk of life: truth to oneself, to one's own innately correct expression. Not all have necessarily found it completely, and perhaps that is not in fact possible or even the point. But each is dedicated, insatiably, to the quest.

Designer/colorist Rosalind Millstone, forever intuitive and inspired, expresses it this way:

I believe that the primary sources of creativity are three: conscious, subconscious and subliminal memories, and they may be present before birth and manifest themselves early on.

I was born in upstate New York in the winter-bound month of February. My first conscious memory is of my father pushing me in a sleigh along a snowy parkway whose bare trees were dark lace-like silhouettes against an opalescent sky.

When the sleigh was taken out of storage for my new brother's first winter, I saw that it was quite like my father's car, built on a child's carriage with runners. It was blue with burnished brass grill and headlights and my father had built it himself. I knew then that it was a gift of love and that love is a stimulus for creativity.

Black, white and blue and the luminescence of a northern winter sky became part of my conscious memory.

Some Canadian beaches are beige sand and huge dunes and at sunset glow pink and orange, and the waters of Lake Ontario turn deepest emerald and the spume becomes so white it achieves a density whose weight might be calculable.

The Tupper Farm...I can't remember where it was...but I can smell the fragrance of grasses under molten sun and close my eyes under golden light that obliterated all detail.

Mostly, I remember water...the colors of a still pond, a clear-water stream over polished stones, the treacherous currents of the Finger Lakes signaling sudden squalls by their mosaic patterns.

All these are of nature, but the impressions of its art on a young child recur again and again and become a part of his essence as an adult.

The stories read, the music heard, the songs sung, the dances danced, and the magic of those who give the gift...when recalled to creator by the child within...are a legacy. Large or small, they impart a grace beyond understanding.

How does this relate to the work? Is it not enough to meld form and function? To please through color and material? To comply with period, show concern for detailing? If the client is pleased and we are pleased are we not entitled to the kudos and accolades? After all, we have conceived it. We have controlled it. We have brought it to fruition.

But what if, through interview or the working of the design process, we can reach the child and his wonder in seeing and his delight in the newly known? Could we not then create, with his essence and ours, not only a thing of beauty but a joy forever?

I've always carried the idea that one is happiest when surrounded by one's toys. My own house is filled with toys…art and artifacts from all over the world, wearable art everywhere…not really toys, but they are to me. And wherever I work, it's the same, simple, basic items sparking and refueling my creativity. These building blocks are key to my work. For example, when I was working in architect Jon Jerde's office to create the color scheme for Westside Center in Westwood, California, I found it very difficult to work with small chips of tile. So I had these large blocks made with each side painted a different color, and I was then able to approach this building as a child might—with blocks. And all the colors fell into place, the palette becoming a joy to work with.

Architects and Designers Who Have Empowered This Book

David Weingarten and Lucia Howard
Ace Architects
The Leviathan
330 Second Street, No. 1
Oakland, California 94607
Tel: (510) 452-0775
Fax: (510) 452-1175

Cleo Baldon
Galper/Baldon Associates
723 Ocean Front Walk
Venice, California 90291
Tel: (310) 392-3992
Fax: (310) 392-9858

Robert E. Barry
Barry Design Associates, Inc.
11601 Wilshire Boulevard, Suite 102
Los Angeles, California 90025
Tel: (310) 478-6081
Fax: (310) 312-9926

Thomas Bartlett
Thomas Bartlett Interiors
P.O. Box 2499
Yountville, California 94599
Tel: (707) 944-2722
Fax: (707) 963-3649

Michael Bedner
Hirsch/Bedner and Associates
3216 Nebraska Avenue
Santa Monica, California 90404
Tel: (310) 829-9087
Fax: (310) 453-1182

Sig Bergamin
Sig Bergamin Interiors, Inc.
29 East 69th Street
New York, New York 10021
Tel: (212) 861-4515
Fax: (212) 861-3667

Erika Brunson
Erika Brunson Design Associates
903 Westbourne Drive
Los Angeles, California 90069
Tel: (310) 652-1970
Fax: (310) 652-2381

Anna Castelli Ferrieri
Corsa de Porta Romana 87/B
20122 Milano
Italy
Tel: 39-2-551-0451
Fax: 39-2-545-2716

Francois Catroux
20 Rue du Faubourg Saint Honore
75008 Paris, France
Tel: 1-42-66-69-25
Fax: 1-42-66-32-86

Steve Chase
Steve Chase Associates
70-005 39th Avenue
Rancho Mirage, California 92270
Tel: (619) 324-4602
Fax: (619) 328-3006

Clodagh
Clodagh Design International
365 First Avenue
New York, New York 10010
Tel: (212) 673-9202
Fax: (212) 614-9125

Jill I. Cole, Principal
Cole Martinez Curtis and Associates
308 Washington Street
Marina del Rey
California 90292
Tel: (310) 827-7200
Fax: (310) 822-5803

Orlando Diaz-Azcuy
Orlando Diaz-Azcuy Designs
45 Maiden Lane
San Francisco, California 94108
Tel: (415) 362-4500
Fax: (415) 788-2311

Paul Draper
Paul Draper and Associates
4106 Swiss Avenue
Dallas, Texas 75204
Tel: (214) 824-8352
Fax: (214) 824-0932

Steven Ehrlich
Steven Ehrlich Architects
1600 Main Street
Venice, California 90291
Tel: (310) 399-7711
Fax: (310) 399-7712

Rand Elliott, AIA
Elliott + Associates Architects
6709 North Classen, Suite 101
Oklahoma City, Oklahoma 73116
Tel: (405) 843-9554
Fax: (405) 843-9607

Arthur Gensler, FAIA
Gensler and Associates Architects
550 Kearney Street
San Francisco, California 94108
Tel: (415) 433-3700
Fax: (415) 627-3737

José Manuel Gomez Vasquez Aldana
Gomez Vasquez Aldana & Asociados
Aurelio Ortega 764
Zapopan, Jalisco, Mexico
Tel: 656-43-43
Fax: 656-40-87

Jacques Grange
118 Rue de Faubourg Saint-Honore
75008 Paris, France
Tel: 1-47-42-47-34
Fax: 1-42-66-24-17

Victoria Hagan
Feldman-Hagan Interiors
22 East 72nd Street
New York, New York 10021
Tel: (212) 472-1290
Fax: (212) 794-3624

Donald Hensman, FAIA
Buff, Smith & Hensman Architects &
Associates
1450 West Colorado
Pasadena, California 91105
Tel: (818) 795-6464
Fax: (818) 795-0961

Agustin Hernandez Navarro, Arquitecto
Bosques de Acacilas, No. 61
Col. Bosques de las Lomas
Mexico 10 D. F. CP. 11700
Tel: 596-15-54
Fax: 596-17-10

Richard Himmel, FASID
1800 Merchandise Mart Plaza
Chicago, Illinois 60654
Tel: (312) 527-5700
Fax: (312) 527-2169

Howard Hirsch
Hirsch/Bedner and Associates
3216 Nebraska Avenue
Santa Monica, California 90404
Tel: (310) 829-9087
Fax: (310) 453-1182

Allison A. Holland, ASID
Creative Decorating
168 Poloke Place
Honolulu, Hawaii 96822
Tel: (808) 955-1465
Fax: (808) 533-6067

Motoko Ishii
President
Motoko Ishii Lighting Design, Inc.
Meikei Building, 6 Rokuban-Cho
Chiyoda-ku, Tokyo, Japan
Tel: (03) 3264-6410
Fax: (03) 3265-6360

Toyo Ito
Toyo Ito & Associates, Architects
Fujiya Building
1-19-4 Shibuya
Shibuya-ku, Tokyo 150, Japan
Tel: (03) 3409-5822
Fax: (03) 3409-5969

Charles Jacobsen
Charles Jacobsen, Inc.
Pacific Design Center G679
8687 Melrose Avenue
West Hollywood, California 90069
Tel: (310) 652-1188
Fax: (310) 652-2555

Noel Jeffrey
Noel Jeffrey, Inc.
215 East 58th Street
New York, New York 10022
Tel: (212) 935-7775
Fax: (212) 935-8280

Dennis Jenkins, ASID, IBD
5813 Southwest 68th Street
South Miami, Florida 33143
Tel: (305) 665-6960
Fax: (305) 573-1744

James F. Jereb, Ph.D.
Tribal Design
1001 East Alameda
Santa Fe, New Mexico 87501
Tel: (505) 989-8765

Scott Johnson
Johnson Fain Pereira Associates
6100 Wilshire Boulevard
Los Angeles, California 90046
Tel: (213) 933-8341
Fax: (213) 933-3120

Tessa Kennedy, ISID
Tessa Kennedy Design, Ltd.
Studio 5
91/97 Freston Road
London W11 4BD
England
Tel: 071-221-4546
Fax: 071-229-2899

Kenneth Ko
Kenneth Ko Design Ltd.
15/F On Wah Ind. Bldg.
41-43, Au Pui Wan Street
Fo Tan, Shatin, Hong Kong
Tel: (852) 604-9494
Fax: (852) 694-1016

Barbara Lazaroff
Imaginings Interior Design
805 North Sierra Drive
Beverly Hills, California 90210
Tel: (310) 276-7939
Fax: (310) 275-9443

Ricardo Legorreta
Legorreta Arquitectos
Palacio de Versalles, #285-A
Lomas Reforma
Mexico, D.F. 11000
Tel: 251-96-98
Fax: 596-61-62

Sally Sirkin Lewis
J. Robert Scott & Associates, Inc.
8727 Melrose Avenue
Los Angeles, California 90069
Tel: (310) 659-4910
Fax: (310) 659-4994

Robert Frank McAlpine
Robert Frank McAlpine
Architecture, Inc.
Sabel Mansion
644 South Perry Street
Montgomery, Alabama 36104

Donald Maxcy, IBD, ASID
Donald Maxcy Design Associates
439 Webster Street
Monterey, California, 93940
Tel: (408) 649-6582
Fax: (408) 649-0519

Joszi Meskan, ASID
Joszi Meskan Associates
479 Ninth Street
San Francisco, California 94103
Tel: (415) 431-0500
Fax: (415) 431-9339

Rosalind Millstone
1220 Loma Vista Drive
Beverly Hills, California 90210
Tel: (310) 271-6339

Vicente Navarro
Cirilo Amoros 85
46004 Valencia, Spain
Tel: 6-373-6293
Fax: 6-395-0335

James Northcutt
James Northcutt Associates
717 North La Cienega Boulevard
Los Angeles, California 90069
Tel: (310) 659-8595
Fax: (310) 659-7120

Antti Nurmesniemi
Studio Nurmesniemi Ky
Hopeasalmentie 27
00570 Helsinki, Finland
Tel: 358 (9) 0-684-7056
Fax: 358 (9) 0-684-8325

Carol Olten
W. Rabbit
7245 Eads Avenue
La Jolla, California 92037
Tel: (619) 454-3660

Gerald Pascal and Carlos Pascal
Pascal Arquitectos
Atlaltunco #99
San Miguel Tecamachalco
Naucalpan, Estado de Mexico
C. P. 53970
Tel: (525) 294-23-71
Fax: (525) 294-85-13

Alie Chang Paul
Alie Design, Inc.
222 Amalfi Drive
Santa Monica, California 90401
Tel: (310) 459-1081
Fax: (310) 459-8530

Antoine Predock
Antoine Predock Architect
300 12th Street, N.W.
Albuquerque, New Mexico 87102
Tel: (505) 843-7390
Fax: (505) 243-6254

Bart Prince
Bart Prince Architect
3501 Monte Vista, N.E.
Albuquerque, New Mexico 87106
Tel: (505) 256-1961
Fax: (505) 268-9045

John F. Saladino
John F. Saladino, Inc.
305 East 63rd Street
New York, New York 10021
Tel: (212) 752-2440
Fax: (212) 838-4933

Louis Shuster
Shuster Design Associates
1401 E. Broward Boulevard, Suite 103
Ft. Lauderdale, Florida 33301
Tel: (305) 462-6400
Fax: (305) 462-6408

Irwin N. Stroll
Irwin N. Stroll & Associates, Inc.
11770 Pacific Coast Highway
Malibu, California 90265
Tel: (310) 657-0741

Imogen Taylor
Sibyl Colefax and John Fowler
39 Brook Street
London W1Y 2JE
England
Tel: 071-493-2231
Fax: 071-355-4037

Margaret I. McCurry, FAIA
Stanley Tigerman, FAIA
Tigerman McCurry Architects
444 North Wells, Suite 206
Chicago, Illinois 60610
Tel: (312) 644-5880
Fax: (312) 644-3750

Massimo and Lella Vignelli
Vignelli Associates
475 Tenth Avenue
New York, New York 10018
Tel: (212) 244-1919
Fax: (212) 967-4961

Lynn Wilson
Lynn Wilson Associates International
111 Majorca Avenue
Coral Gables, Florida 33134
Tel: (305) 442-4041
Fax: (305) 443-4276

Trisha Wilson
Wilson & Associates
3811 Turtle Creek Boulevard, 15th Floor
Dallas, Texas 75219-4419
Tel: (214) 521-6753
Fax: (214) 521-0207

James Wines
SITE
65 Bleecker Street
New York, New York 10012
Tel: (212) 254-8300
Fax: (212) 353-3086

Vicente Wolf
Vicente Wolf Associates, Inc.
333 West 39 Street
New York, New York 10018
Tel: (212) 465-0590
Fax: (212) 465-0639

George Yabu
Glenn Pushelberg
Yabu Pushelberg
55 Booth Avenue
Toronto, Canada M4M 2M3
Tel: (416) 778-9779
Fax: (416) 778-9747

ACKNOWLEDGMENTS

With much gratitude to the following people for their assistance and support:

Sally K. Backlin
Carla Breeze
Janice Feldman
Julie Goodman
Jody Greenwald
Lena Torslow Hansen
Akira Hashimoto
Marcia W. Hobbs
Pina Manzone
Judy Szyf
Cristina Villo